THE COOK'S ENCYCLOPEDIA OF
CHICKEN

THE COOK'S ENCYCLOPEDIA OF
CHICKEN

CONTRIBUTING EDITOR: LINDA FRASER

LORENZ BOOKS

This edition first published by Lorenz Books
27 West 20th Street, New York, NY 10011

LORENZ BOOKS are available for bulk purchase for sales promotion
and for premium use. For details, write or call the sales director,
Lorenz Books, 27 West 20th Street, New York, NY 10011;
(800) 354-9657

www.lorenzbooks.com

© Anness Publishing Limited 1996, 2000

Lorenz Books is an imprint of Anness Publishing Inc.

Publisher: Joanna Lorenz
Cookery Editor: Rosemary Wilkinson
Copy Editor: Rosie Hankin
Designer: Bill Mason
Recipes: Catherine Atkinson, Alex Barker, Carla Capalbo, Maxine Clark, Andi Clevely, Christine France,
Carole Handslip, Sarah Gates, Shirley Gill, Norma MacMillan, Sue Maggs, Katherine Richmond,
Jenny Stacey, Ruby Le Bois, Liz Trigg, Hilaire Walden, Laura Washburn, Steven Wheeler
Photographers: Karl Adamson, Edward Allwright, Steve Baxter, James Duncan, John Freeman,
Michelle Garrett, Amanda Heywood, Don Last
Stylists: Madeleine Brehaut, Hilary Guy, Blake Minton, Kirsty Rawlings, Fiona Tillett
Food for Photography: Marilyn Forbes, Carole Handslip, Jane Hartshorn, Cara Hobday,
Beverly LeBlanc, Wendy Lee, Lucie McKelvie, Jenny Shapter, Elizabeth Silver, Jane Stevenson,
Liz Trigg, Elizabeth Wolf-Cohen
Illustrator: Anna Koska

Previously published as *The Ultimate Chicken Cookbook*

Printed and bound in China
Updated © 2001
3 5 7 9 10 8 6 4

CONTENTS

~

Introduction

Chicken is popular with children and adults alike. It is versatile and economical, and can be cooked with a wide variety of ingredients and flavors. It is low in fat and quick to cook, with very little wastage.

Chicken can be bought in many forms: whole, quartered or cut into thighs, drumsticks, breasts and wings, with or without bones and skin, which makes preparation very easy. Ground chicken can be found at some large supermarkets, but the skinned flesh can be ground quickly in a food processor. Although it is convenient to buy portions individually packed, it is expensive. It is much cheaper to buy a whole chicken and prepare it yourself and cheaper still to buy a frozen chicken and defrost it thoroughly before using. To get the best results from a frozen bird, allow it to thaw slowly in a cool place overnight or until completely defrosted. Many types of chicken are available, such as free-range and corn-fed (with yellow skin) and all are full of flavor. Some have added herbs and flavorings, and others are self-basting with either butter or olive oil injected into the flesh. This helps to keep the flesh succulent. Rock Cornish hens are the smallest domestic birds available; they weigh from ¾ to 2 pounds. Sometimes found fresh, they are always available frozen. Chickens weigh from 2-6 pounds, and turkey up to 25 or more, so there's a bird to suit every family and occasion.

The recipes in this book are mostly based on a family of four people, but they can be easily halved for two or doubled for eight. There are chapters on soups, salads and pies as well as one pot meals, midweek meals and hot and spicy dishes to provide you with a best-ever chicken meal for every occasion.

Choosing a Chicken

*A fresh chicken should have a plump
breast and the skin should be
creamy in color. The tip of the breast
bone should be pliable.*

*A bird's dressed weight is taken
after plucking and drawing and may
include the giblets (neck, gizzard,
heart and liver). A frozen chicken
must be thawed slowly in the fridge
or a cool room. Never put it in hot
water, as this will toughen the flesh
and is dangerous as it allows
bacteria to multiply.*

Rock Cornish hens
These are four to six weeks old and
weigh 1–1¼ pounds. One is enough
for one person.

Broiling chickens
These are eight to ten weeks old and
weigh 1¾–2 pounds. One will serve
two people. Poussins are best roasted,
broiled or pot-roasted.

Boiling fowl
These are about twelve
months old and over
and weigh between
4–6 pounds. They
require long, slow
cooking, around 2–3
hours, to make them
tender.

Roasters
These birds are about six to twelve
months old and weigh 3–6 pounds.
One will feed a family.

Corn-fed chickens
These are generally more expensive.
They usually weigh 2½–3 pounds.

Frying chickens
These birds are about three months
old and weigh 2–3 pounds. One will
serve three to four people.

Cuts of Chicken

Chicken pieces are available pre-packaged in various forms. If you do not want to buy a whole bird, you can make your choice from the many cuts on the market.

Some cooking methods are especially suited to specific cuts of poultry.

Liver
This makes a wonderful addition to pâtés or to salads.

Drumstick
The drumstick is a firm favorite for barbecuing or frying, either in batter or rolled in breadcrumbs.

Wing
The wing does not supply much meat, and is often barbecued or fried.

Skinless boneless thigh
This makes tasks such as stuffing and rolling much quicker, as it is already skinned and dis-jointed.

Thigh
The thigh is suitable for casseroling and other slow-cooking methods.

Breast
The tender white meat can be simply cooked in butter, or can be stuffed for extra flavor.

Ground chicken
This is not as strongly flavored as, say, ground beef, but it may be used as a substitute in some recipes.

Leg
This comprises the drumstick and thigh. Large pieces with bones, such as this, are suitable for slow-cooking, such as casseroling or poaching.

Trussing Poultry

Trussing holds a bird together during cooking so that it keeps a neat, attractive shape. If the bird is stuffed, trussing prevents the stuffing from falling out. You can truss with strong string or poultry skewers.

An alternative to the method shown here is to use a long trussing needle and fine cotton string: make two passes, in alternate directions, through the body at the open end, from wing to wing, and tie. Then pass the needle through the pope's nose and tie the string around the ends of the drumsticks.

Remove trussing before serving.

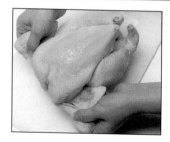

1 For an unstuffed bird: set it breast down and pull the neck skin over the neck opening. Turn the bird breast up and fold the wing tips back, over the skin, to secure behind the shoulders.

2 Press the legs down firmly and into the breast. If there is a band of skin across the pope's nose, fold back the ends of the drumsticks and tuck them under the skin.

3 Otherwise, cross the knuckle ends of the drumsticks or bring them tightly together. Loop a length of string several times around the drumstick ends, tie a knot and trim off excess string.

4 For a stuffed bird: fold the wing tips back as above. After stuffing the neck end, fold the flap of skin over the opening and secure it with a skewer, then fold over the wing tips.

5 Put any stuffing or flavorings (herbs, lemon halves, apple quarters and so on) in the body cavity, then secure the ends of the drumsticks as above, tying in the pope's nose, too.

6 Or, the cavity opening can be closed with skewers: insert two or more skewers across the opening, threading them through the skin several times.

7 Lace the skewers together with string. Tie the drumsticks together over the skewers.

STUFFING TIPS

Only use stuffing that is cool, not hot or chilled. Pack it loosely in the bird and cook any leftovers separately. Stuff poultry just before cooking. Do not stuff the body cavity of a large bird because this could inhibit heat penetration, and thus harmful bacteria may not be destroyed.

Roasting Poultry

Where would family gatherings be without the time-honored roast bird? Beyond the favorite chicken, all types of poultry can be roasted – from Rock Cornish hens to large turkeys. However, older, tougher birds are better pot-roasted.

SIMPLE ROAST CHICKEN
◆

Squeeze the juice from a halved lemon over a 3–3¹/₂-pound chicken, then push the lemon halves into the body cavity. Smear 1 tablespoon softened butter over the breast. Roast in a 375°F oven for about 1¹/₄ hours. Skim all fat from the roasting juices, then add ¹/₂ cup water and bring to a boil, stirring well to mix in the browned bits. Season with salt and pepper, and serve this sauce with the chicken.

Serves 4.

1 Wipe the bird inside and out with damp paper towels, stuff, if desired and truss it. Spread the breast of chicken with soft butter or oil; bard a lean game bird; prick the skin of duck or goose.

2 Set the bird breast up on a rack in a small roasting pan or shallow baking dish. If you are roasting a lean game bird, set the bird in the pan breast down.

 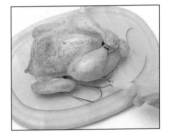

3 Roast the bird, basting every 10 minutes after the first 30 minutes with the juices and fat in the pan. If browning too quickly, cover with foil.

4 Put the bird on a carving board and let it rest for at least 15 minutes before serving. Meanwhile make a simple sauce or gravy with the juices in the pan.

ROASTING TIMES FOR POULTRY

Note: Cooking times given here are for unstuffed birds.
For stuffed birds, add 20 minutes to the total roasting time.

ROCK CORNISH HEN	1–1¹/₂ pounds	1–1¹/₄ hours at 350°F
CHICKEN	2¹/₂–3 pounds	1–1¹/₄ hours at 375°F
	3¹/₂–4 pounds	1¹/₄–2 hours at 375°F
	4¹/₂–5 pounds	1¹/₂–2 hours at 375°F
	5–6 pounds	1³/₄–2¹/₂ hours at 375°F
DUCK	3–5 pounds	1³/₄–2¹/₄ hours at 400°F
GOOSE	8–10 pounds	2¹/₂–3 hours at 350°F
	10–12 pounds	3–3¹/₂ hours at 350°F
TURKEY	6–8 pounds	3–3¹/₂ hours at 325°F
(whole bird)	8–12 pounds	3–4 hours at 325°F
	12–16 pounds	4–5 hours at 325°F
TURKEY	4–6 pounds	1¹/₂–2¹/₄ hours at 325°F
(whole breast)	6–8 pounds	2¹/₄–3¹/₄ hours at 325°F

PROTECT & FLAVOR
◆

Before roasting, loosen the skin on the breast by gently easing it away from the flesh with your fingers. Press in softened butter – mixed with herbs or garlic for extra flavor – and smooth back the skin. To bard poultry, cover the breast with slices of bacon before roasting.

Cutting Up Poultry

Although chickens and other poultry are sold already cut into halves, quarters, breasts, thighs and drumsticks, sometimes it makes sense to buy a whole bird and to do the job yourself. That way you can prepare four larger pieces or eight smaller ones, depending on the recipe, and you can cut the pieces so the backbone and other bony bits (which can be saved for stock) are not included. Also, a whole bird is cheaper to buy than pieces.

A sharp knife and sturdy kitchen scissors or poultry shears make the job of cutting up poultry very easy.

1 With the sharp knife, cut through the skin on one side of the body down to where the thigh joins the body. Bend the leg out away from the body and twist it to break the ball and socket joint.

2 Hold the leg out away from the body and cut through the ball and socket joint, taking the "oyster meat" from the backbone with the leg. Repeat on the other side.

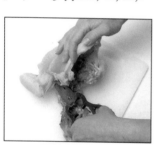

3 To separate the breast from the back, cut through the flap of skin just below the rib cage, cutting towards the neck. Pull the breast and back apart, cutting through the joints that connect them. Reserve the back for stock.

4 Turn the whole breast over, skin side down. Take one side of the breast in each hand and bend back firmly so the breastbone pops free. Loosen the bone on both sides with your fingers and, using a knife to help, remove it.

5 Cut the breast lengthwise in half, cutting through the wishbone. You now have 2 breasts with wings attached and 2 leg portions.

6 For 8 pieces, cut each breast in half at an angle so that some breast is included with each wing. Trim off any protruding bones.

7 With the knife, cut each leg portion through the ball and socket joint to separate the thigh and drumstick.

Boning a Chicken

For the purpose of stuffing, and to make carving simple, it is essential to bone a chicken. Use a sharp knife with a short blade. Work in short, scraping movements, keeping the knife against the bone at all times, to leave the carcass clean.

1 Remove any trussing string. Cut off the wing tips (pinions) and discard. With a short-bladed, sharp knife, cut the skin along the underside (backbone) of the chicken. Carefully work the skin and flesh away from the carcass with the knife until the leg joints are exposed.

2 Cut the sinew between the ball and socket joints. This sinew joins the thigh bones and wings to the carcass.

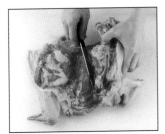

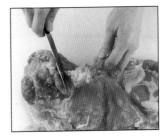

3 Holding the rib cage away from the chicken body, carefully scrape the breastbone clean and cut the carcass away from the skin. Take great care not to cut through the skin, or the stuffing will burst out of the hole.

4 Take hold of the thigh bone in one hand, and with the knife scrape the flesh down the bone to the next joint.

5 Cut around the joint and continue cleaning the drumstick until the whole leg bone is free. Repeat with the other leg and both the wings. Lay the chicken flat and turn the flesh of the legs and wings inside the chicken. Flatten the flesh neatly so the bird is ready to stuff.

HANDLING RAW POULTRY

Raw poultry may harbor harmful organisms, such as salmonella bacteria, so it is vital to take care in its preparation. Always wash your hands, cutting board, knife and poultry shears in hot soapy water before and after handling poultry. If possible, use a cutting board that can be washed at a high temperature in a dishwasher, and always keep a cutting board just for the preparation of raw poultry. Thaw frozen poultry completely before cooking.

Butterflying Poultry

Whole chickens, Rock Cornish hens, guinea fowl and game birds can be split in half and opened flat like a book to resemble the wings of a butterfly. They will then cook evenly under the broiler or on a grill. A heavy knife can be used to split the bird, but sturdy kitchen scissors or poultry shears are easier to handle.

1 Set the bird breast down. Cut through the skin and rib cage along one side of the backbone, working from the tail end to the neck. Repeat on the other side of the backbone to cut it free. Keep the backbone for stock, if desired.

2 Turn the bird breast up. With the heel of your hand, press firmly on the breastbone to break it and flatten the breast.

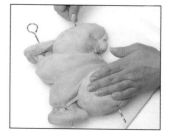

3 Fold the wing tips back behind the shoulders. Thread a long metal skewer through one wing and the top of the breast and out through the other wing.

4 Thread a second skewer through the thighs and bottom of the breast. These skewers will keep the bird flat during cooking and will make it easy to turn over.

TESTING POULTRY

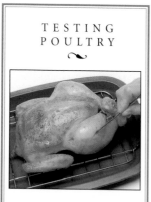

Overcooked poultry is dry, tough and tasteless, so knowing when a bird is done is crucial. The most reliable test for a whole bird is to insert a meat thermometer deep into the thigh meat (the internal temperature should be 175°F). Without a thermometer, you can test by piercing the thigh with a skewer or the tip of a knife; the juices that run out should be clear, not pink. Or, lift the bird with a long two-pronged fork and tilt it so you can check the color of the juices that run out of the cavity into the roasting pan. Pieces of poultry, particularly breasts, can be tested by pressing them with a finger; the meat should be firm but still slightly springy.

BROILING TIMES FOR POULTRY

Note: Cook 4–6 inches from the heat; thinner pieces, less than 1 inch nearer the heat.
If the poultry seems to be browning too quickly, turn down the heat slightly.

ROCK CORNISH HEN, BUTTERFLIED	20–25 minutes
CHICKEN, BROILER OR FRYER, SPLIT IN HALF OR BUTTERFLIED	25–30 minutes
ROASTING CHICKEN, SPLIT IN HALF OR BUTTERFLIED	30–40 minutes
CHICKEN BREAST, DRUMSTICK, THIGH	30–35 minutes
SKINLESS BONELESS CHICKEN BREAST	10–12 minutes
BONELESS DUCK BREAST	10–12 minutes

Making Poultry Stock

A good homemade poultry stock is invaluable in the kitchen. It is simple and economical to make, and can be stored in the freezer for up to 6 months. If poultry giblets are available, add them (except the livers) with the wings.

Makes about 10 cups

2^1/$_2$–3 pounds poultry wings, backs and
   necks (chicken, turkey, etc)
2 onions, unpeeled, quartered
7 pints cold water
2 carrots, coarsely chopped
2 celery stalks, with leaves if possible,
   coarsely chopped
a small handful of fresh parsley
a few fresh thyme sprigs or
^{3}/$_4$ teaspoon dried thyme
1 or 2 bay leaves
10 black peppercorns, lightly crushed

1 Combine the poultry wings, backs and necks and the onions in a stockpot. Cook over moderate heat until the poultry and onion pieces are lightly browned, stirring from time to time so they color evenly.

2 Add the water and stir well to mix in the sediment on the bottom of the pot. Bring to a boil and skim off the impurities as they rise to the surface of the stock.

3 Add the remaining ingredients. Partially cover the stockpot and gently simmer the stock for about 3 hours.

4 Strain the stock into a bowl and allow to cool, then refrigerate.

FRUGAL STOCK

∽

Stock can be made from the bones and carcasses of roasted poultry, cooked with vegetables and flavorings. Save the carcasses in a plastic bag in the freezer until you have three or four, then make stock. It may not have quite as rich a flavor as stock made from a whole bird or fresh wings, backs and necks, but it will still taste fresher and less salty than stock made from a commercial cube.

5 When cold, carefully remove the layer of fat that will have settled on the surface.

STOCK TIPS

∽

If desired, use a whole bird for making stock instead of wings, backs and necks. A boiling fowl, if available, will give wonderful flavor and provide meat to use in salads, sandwiches, soups and casseroles.

No salt is added to stock because as the stock reduces, the flavor becomes concentrated and the saltiness increases. Add salt to dishes which contain the stock.

Making Poultry Sautés

A sauté combines frying and braising, producing especially succulent results. It is a method suitable for pieces of poultry as well as for small whole birds such as quails and Rock Cornish hens.

As with frying, the poultry should be dried thoroughly with paper towels before cooking, to make sure that it browns quickly and evenly.

1 Heat a little oil, a mixture of oil and butter, or clarified butter in a heavy frying or sauté pan.

2 Add the poultry and fry over medium heat until it is golden brown, turning to color evenly.

COUNTRY CHICKEN SAUTE

Cook 6 ounces chopped bacon in 2 teaspoons oil over moderately high heat until lightly colored. Remove bacon and reserve. Dredge a 3¹/₂-pound chicken, cut into eight pieces, in seasoned flour. Fry chicken pieces in the bacon fat until evenly browned. Add 3 tablespoons of dry white wine and 1 cup poultry stock. Bring to a boil and add 8 ounces quartered mushrooms sautéed in 1 tablespoon of butter and the reserved bacon. Cover and cook over low heat for 20–25 minutes, or until the chicken is tender.
Serves 4.

3 Add any liquid and flavorings called for in the recipe. Bring to a boil, then cover and reduce the heat to medium low. Continue cooking gently until the poultry is done, turning the pieces or birds over once or twice.

4 If the recipe requires it remove the poultry from the pan and keep it warm while finishing the sauce. This can be as simple as boiling the cooking juices to reduce them or adding butter or cream for a richer result.

5 To thicken the cooking juices use equal weights of butter and flour mashed together. Use 1 ounce of this "beurre manié" to 1 cup liquid. Add small pieces gradually to the hot juices and whisk until mixture is smooth.

6 Another method of thickening cooking juices is to use cornstarch. Blend 2 teaspoons cornstarch with 1 tablespoon water and add to 1 cup juices. Boil, whisking, for 2–3 minutes, until the sauce is syrupy.

Frying Chicken

Fried chicken is justifiably popular – crisp and brown outside and tender and juicy within. It's a quick and easy cooking method that can be applied to pieces of rabbit and hare and small turkey joints, too.

Dry the pieces thoroughly with paper towels before frying. If they are at all wet, they will not brown properly. If the recipe suggests it, lightly coat the pieces with egg and crumbs or with a batter.

SUCCULENT FRIED CHICKEN

Mix 1 cup milk with 1 beaten egg in a shallow dish. On a sheet of waxed paper combine 1¼ cups all-purpose flour, 1 teaspoon paprika, and some salt and pepper. One at a time, dip eight chicken pieces in the egg mixture and turn them to coat all over. Then dip in the seasoned flour and shake off any excess. Deep-fry for 25–30 minutes, turning the pieces so they brown and cook evenly. Drain on paper towels and serve very hot.
Serves 4.

1 To pan-fry, heat oil, a mixture of oil and butter, or clarified butter in a large, heavy-bottomed frying pan over medium heat. When very hot, add the chicken pieces, skin-side down.

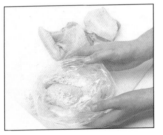

3 To deep-fry, dip the pieces into a mixture of milk and beaten egg and coat lightly with seasoned flour. Allow coating to set for 20 minutes before frying. (Or, dip the pieces in batter before frying.)

5 With a spatula or tongs, lower the chicken pieces into the oil, a few at a time. Deep-fry, turning during cooking, until they are golden brown all over and cooked.

2 Fry until deep golden brown all over, turning the pieces during cooking. Fry until the pieces are thoroughly cooked. Remove pieces of breast before drumsticks and thighs. Drain on paper towels.

4 Half fill a deep pan with vegetable oil. Heat it to 365°F. You can test the temperature with a cube of bread; if it takes 50 seconds to brown, the oil is at the right temperature.

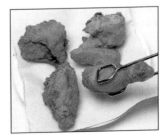

6 Drain on paper towels and serve hot. If you want to keep a batch of fried chicken hot while frying the rest, put it, uncovered, into a low oven.

Poaching, Casseroling & Braising

SIMPLE CHICKEN STOCK

This all-purpose chicken stock may be used as the basis for a wonderful homemade soup.

1 Put the giblets (the neck, gizzard and heart, but not the liver, as it makes stock bitter), or the carcass from a cooked chicken, into a pan and just cover with cold water.

2 Add a quartered onion, carrot, bouquet garni (bay leaf, thyme and parsley) and a few pepper-corns. Bring to a boil, cover and simmer gently for 1–2 hours.

3 Remove any scum that rises to the surface with a large slotted spoon. Alternatively, make the stock when you cook the chicken, by putting the giblets in the roast-ing pan around the chicken with the onion and herbs and just enough water to keep them from burning.

4 When the stock has cooled and set, carefully remove the fat from the surface with a spoon. Add salt to taste when using the stock.

POACHING

Poaching is a very gentle cooking method and produces stock for making a sauce afterwards.

1 Put the chicken into a flame-proof casserole with a bouquet garni (bay leaf, thyme and parsley), carrot and onion.

2 Cover with water and add salt and peppercorns. Bring to a boil, cover and simmer for about 1 1/2 hours, or until tender.

3 Cool in the liquid or lift out, shred, and combine with a white sauce.

BRAISING

This method can be used for whole chickens and pieces and is ideal for strongly-flavored meat.

1 Heat olive oil in a flameproof casserole and lightly fry a chicken or pieces until golden.

2 Remove the chicken and stir-fry 1 pound of diced vegetables (carrots, onions, celery and turnips), until soft.

3 Replace the chicken, cover tightly, and cook very slowly on the stovetop or in a preheated oven at 325°F, until tender.

CASSEROLING

This slow-cooking method is good for large chicken joints with bones, or more mature meat.

1 Heat olive oil in a flameproof casserole and brown the chicken joints.

2 Add some stock, wine or a mixture of both to a depth of 1 inch. Add seasonings and herbs, cover, and cook on the stovetop or in the oven, as for braising, for 1–1 1/2 hours, or until tender.

3 Add a selection of lightly stir-fried vegetables such as baby onions, mushrooms, carrots and small new potatoes about halfway through the cooking time.

Five Stuffings for Chicken

BASIC HERB STUFFING

INGREDIENTS

1 small onion, finely chopped
1 tablespoon butter
2 cups fresh breadcrumbs
1 tablespoon chopped fresh parsley
1 teaspoon mixed dried herbs
1 egg, beaten
salt and black pepper

Cook the onion gently in the
butter until tender. Allow to cool.
Add to the remaining ingredients and then mix thoroughly.
Season well with salt and pepper.

VARIATIONS

*Any of these ingredients may be
added to the basic recipe to vary the
flavor of the stuffing, depending on
what you have in your fridge and
cupboards at home.*

1 celery stalk, finely chopped
1 small eating apple, diced
$1/2$ cup chopped walnuts
    or almonds
1 tablespoon raisins
$1/4$ cup chopped dried prunes
    or apricots
$2/3$ cup mushrooms, finely chopped
grated rind of $1/2$ orange or lemon
$1/2$ cup pine nuts
2 strips bacon, chopped

APRICOT AND ORANGE STUFFING

INGREDIENTS

1 tablespoon butter
1 small onion, finely chopped
2 cups fresh breadcrumbs
$1/4$ cup finely chopped dried
    apricots
grated rind of $1/2$ orange
1 small egg, beaten
1 tablespoon chopped fresh
    parsley
salt and black pepper

Heat the butter in a frying pan
and cook the onion gently
until tender.
Allow to cool slightly, and add
to the rest of the ingredients.
Mix until thoroughly combined
and season with salt and pepper.

RAISIN AND NUT STUFFING

INGREDIENTS

2 cups fresh breadcrumbs
$1/3$ cup raisins
$1/2$ cup walnuts, almonds, pistachios or
    pine nuts
1 tablespoon chopped fresh
    parsley
1 teaspoon chopped mixed herbs
1 small egg, beaten
2 tablespoons melted butter
salt and black pepper

Mix all the ingredients
together thoroughly.
Season well with
salt and pepper.

Raisin and Nut Stuffing

PARSLEY, LEMON AND THYME STUFFING

INGREDIENTS

2 cups fresh breadcrumbs
2 tablespoons butter
1 tablespoon chopped fresh parsley
$1/2$ teaspoon dried thyme
grated rind of $1/4$ lemon
1 strip lean bacon, chopped
1 small egg, beaten
salt and black pepper

Mix all the ingredients together
to combine them thoroughly.

Parsley, Lemon and Thyme Stuffing

SAUSAGE STUFFING

INGREDIENTS

1 tablespoon butter
1 small onion, finely chopped
2 strips lean bacon, chopped
8 ounces sausage meat
$1/2$ teaspoon mixed dried herbs
salt and black pepper

Heat the butter in a frying pan
and cook the onion until tender.
Add the bacon and cook for
5 minutes, then allow to cool.
Add to the remaining ingredients and mix thoroughly.

 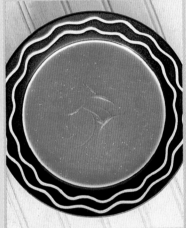 

SOUPS &
APPETIZERS

~

Chicken and Lentil Soup

A chunky soup that makes a good lunchtime dish.

INGREDIENTS

Serves 4

2 tablespoons butter or margarine

1 large carrot, chopped

1 onion, chopped

1 leek, white part only, chopped

1 celery stalk, chopped

4 ounces mushrooms, chopped

3 tablespoons dry white wine

4 cups homemade or canned chicken
    stock

2 teaspoons dried thyme

1 bay leaf

$^1/_2$ cup brown or green lentils

8 ounces cooked chicken, diced

salt and black pepper

1 Melt the butter or margarine in a large saucepan. Add the carrot, onion, leek, celery and mushrooms. Cook for 3–5 minutes, until softened.

2 Stir in the wine and chicken stock. Bring to a boil and skim off any foam that rises to the surface. Add the thyme and bay leaf. Reduce the heat, cover, and simmer for 30 minutes.

3 Add the lentils and continue cooking, covered, for another 30–40 minutes, until they are just tender, stirring the soup from time to time.

4 Stir in the diced chicken and season to taste with salt and pepper. Cook until just heated through. Ladle the soup into bowls and serve hot.

Chicken Vermicelli Soup with Egg Shreds

This light soup can be put together in a matter of minutes and is full of flavor.

Serves 4–6

3 jumbo eggs

2 tablespoons chopped cilantro
  or parsley

6¹/4 cups homemade or canned chicken
  stock

1 cup dried vermicelli or angel
  hair pasta

4 ounces cooked chicken breast, sliced

salt and pepper

1 First make the egg shreds.
Whisk the eggs together in a small bowl and stir in the chopped cilantro or parsley.

2 Heat a small nonstick frying pan and pour in 2–3 table-spoons beaten egg, swirling to cover the bottom evenly. Cook until set. Repeat until all the mixture is used up.

3 Roll each pancake up and slice thinly into shreds. Set aside.

4 Bring the stock to a boil and add the pasta, breaking it into short lengths. Cook for 3–5 minutes, until the pasta is almost tender, then add the chicken, salt and pepper. Heat through for 2–3 minutes, then stir in the egg shreds. Serve immediately.

Cream of Scallion Soup

A meltingly smooth soup of chicken stock, potato and scallions.

INGREDIENTS

Serves 4–6

2 tablespoons butter

1 small onion, chopped

5 ounces scallions, white parts only, chopped

8 ounces potato, peeled and chopped

$2^{1}/_{2}$ cups homemade or canned chicken stock

$1^{1}/_{2}$ cups light cream

salt and white pepper

2 tablespoons lemon juice

chopped scallions or chives, to garnish

1 Melt the butter in a saucepan and add all the onions. Cover and cook over very low heat for about 10 minutes, or until soft.

2 Add the potatoes and the stock. Bring to a boil, cover again, and simmer over medium low heat for 30 minutes. Cool slightly.

3 Purée the soup in a blender or food processor.

4 If serving the soup hot, pour it back into the pan. Add the cream and season. Reheat gently, stirring frequently. Stir in the lemon juice and garnish before serving.

Zucchini Soup with Small Pasta Shells

An attractive and refreshing soup which could be made using cucumber instead of zucchini.

Serves 4–6

4 tablespoons olive or sunflower oil

2 medium onions, finely chopped

6$\frac{1}{4}$ cups homemade or canned chicken stock

2 pounds zucchini

1 cup small pasta for soup

fresh lemon juice

salt and pepper

2 tablespoons chopped fresh chervil

sour cream, to serve

1 Heat the oil in a large saucepan and add the onions. Cover and cook gently for about 20 minutes, until very soft but not colored, stirring occasionally.

2 Add the chicken stock and bring to a boil.

3 Meanwhile grate the zucchini and stir into the boiling stock with the pasta. Turn down the heat and simmer for 15 minutes, until the pasta is tender. Season to taste with lemon juice, salt and pepper.

4 Stir in the chervil and add a swirl of sour cream to serve.

Country Vegetable Soup

To stir things up, vary the vegetables according to the season.

INGREDIENTS

Serves 4

4 tablespoons butter

1 onion, chopped

2 leeks, sliced

2 celery stalks, sliced

2 carrots, sliced

2 small turnips, chopped

4 ripe tomatoes, peeled and chopped

4 cups homemade or canned
   chicken stock

bouquet garni

4 ounces green beans, chopped

salt and pepper

chopped herbs such as tarragon, thyme,
   chives and parsley, to garnish

1 Heat the butter in a large saucepan, add the onion and leeks and cook gently until soft but not colored.

2 Add the celery, carrots and turnips and cook for 3–4 minutes, stirring occasionally. Stir in the tomatoes and stock, add the bouquet garni and simmer for about 20 minutes.

3 Add the beans to the soup and cook until all the vegetables are tender. Season to taste and serve garnished with chopped herbs.

Split Pea and Bacon Soup

In England, another name for this soup is "London Particular," from the dense fogs for which the city used to be notorious. The fogs in turn were called "pea-soupers."

INGREDIENTS

Serves 4

1 tablespoon butter

4 ounces Canadian bacon, chopped

1 large onion, chopped

1 carrot, chopped

1 celery stalk, chopped

$1/2$ cup split peas

5 cups homemade or canned
   chicken stock

2 thick slices firm bread, buttered and
   without crusts

2 slices lean bacon

salt and pepper

1 Heat the butter in a saucepan, add the Canadian bacon and cook until the fat runs. Stir in the onion, carrot and celery and cook for 2–3 minutes.

2 Add the split peas and then the stock. Bring to a boil, stirring occasionally, then cover and simmer for 45–60 minutes.

3 Meanwhile, preheat the oven to 350°F and bake the bread on a baking sheet for about 20 minutes, until crisp and brown, then cut into cubes.

4 Broil the lean bacon until very crisp, then chop finely.

5 When the soup is ready, season to taste and serve hot with chopped bacon and croutons sprinkled on each portion.

Mulligatawny Soup

Mulligatawny (which means "pepper water") was introduced into England in the late eighteenth century, by members of the army and colonial service returning home from India.

INGREDIENTS

Serves 4

4 tablespoons butter or 4 tablespoons
  olive oil
2 large chicken joints, about
  12 ounces each
1 onion, chopped
1 carrot, chopped
1 small turnip, chopped
about 1 tablespoon curry powder, to taste
4 cloves
6 black peppercorns, lightly crushed
$^1/_4$ cup lentils
$3^3/_4$ cups homemade or canned
  chicken stock
$^1/_4$ cup golden raisins
salt and pepper

1 Melt the butter or heat the oil in a large saucepan and brown the chicken over brisk heat. Transfer the chicken onto a plate.

2 Add the onion, carrot and turnip to the pan and cook, stirring occasionally, until lightly colored. Stir in the curry powder, cloves and peppercorns and cook for 1–2 minutes. Add the lentils.

3 Pour in the stock and bring to a boil. Add the golden raisins and chicken and any juices from the plate. Cover and simmer gently for about $1^1/_4$ hours.

COOK'S TIP

Red split lentils will give the best color for this dish, although green or brown lentils could be used, if you prefer.

4 Remove the chicken from the pan and discard the skin and bones. Chop the flesh, return to the soup and reheat. Check and adjust the seasoning before serving the soup piping hot.

Thai Chicken Soup

*This filling and tasty soup is very
quick to prepare and cook.*

INGREDIENTS

Serves 4

1 tablespoon vegetable oil
1 garlic clove, finely chopped
2 boned chicken breasts, about 6 ounces
   each, skinned and chopped
$1/2$ teaspoon ground turmeric
$1/4$ teaspoon hot chili powder
3 ounces creamed coconut
$3^3/4$ cups hot homemade or canned
   chicken stock,
2 tablespoons lemon or lime juice
2 tablespoons crunchy peanut butter
1 cup thread egg noodles, broken into
   small pieces
1 tablespoon scallions, finely chopped
1 tablespoon chopped fresh cilantro
salt and black pepper
2 tablespoons dried coconut and $1/2$ fresh
   red chili, seeded and finely chopped, to
   garnish

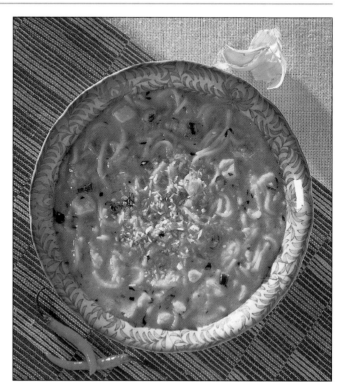

1 Heat the oil in a large pan and
fry the garlic for 1 minute,
until lightly golden. Add the
chicken and spices and stir-fry for
another 3–4 minutes.

2 Crumble the creamed coconut
into the hot chicken stock and
stir until dissolved. Pour onto the
chicken and add the lemon or lime
juice, peanut butter and egg
noodles.

3 Cover the pan and simmer for
about 15 minutes.

4 Add the chopped scallions and
cilantro, then season well and
cook for another 5 minutes.
Meanwhile, place the dried
coconut and chili in a small frying
pan and heat for 2–3 minutes, stirring frequently.

5 Serve the soup in bowls and
sprinkle each one with some
fried coconut and hot chili.

New England Spiced Pumpkin Soup

Pumpkin soup cooked with spices, brown sugar and orange juice.

INGREDIENTS

Serves 4

2 tablespoons butter
1 onion, finely chopped
1 small garlic clove, crushed
1 tablespoon all-purpose flour
pinch of grated nutmeg
$^1/_2$ teaspoon ground cinnamon
3 cups pumpkin, seeded,
   peeled and cubed
$2^1/_2$ cups homemade or canned
   chicken stock
$^2/_3$ cup orange juice
1 teaspoon brown sugar
1 tablespoon vegetable oil
2 slices whole wheat bread without crusts
2 tablespoons sunflower seeds

1 Heat the butter in a large saucepan, add the onion and garlic and fry gently for 4–5 minutes, until softened. Stir in the flour, all the spices and the pumpkin,

2 Cover and cook gently for about 6 minutes, stirring occasionally.

3 Pour in the chicken stock and orange juice and add the brown sugar. Cover and bring to a boil, then reduce the heat and simmer for 20 minutes, until the pumpkin has softened.

4 Pour half of the mixture into a blender or food processor and process until smooth. Return the soup to the pan with the remaining chunky mixture. Season well and heat through, stirring.

5 Meanwhile, make the croutons. Heat the oil in a frying pan, cut the bread into cubes and fry gently until just beginning to brown. Add the sunflower seeds and fry for 1–2 minutes. Drain the croutons and sunflower seeds on paper towels.

6 Serve the soup hot with a few of the croutons and sunflower seeds sprinkled over the top. Serve the rest separately.

Green Pea and Mint Soup

This soup is equally delicious cold. Instead of reheating it after puréeing, let it cool and then chill lightly in the fridge. Stir in the swirl of cream just before serving.

INGREDIENTS

Serves 4

4 tablespoons butter
4 scallions, chopped
4 cups fresh or frozen peas
2¹/2 cups homemade or canned
    chicken stock
2 large mint sprigs
2¹/2 cups milk
pinch of sugar (optional)
salt and pepper
light cream, to serve
small mint sprigs, to garnish

1 Heat the butter in a large saucepan, add the scallions, and cook gently until softened but not colored.

FREEZER NOTE

~

The soup can be frozen for up to two months after step 2. Allow it to thaw in the fridge before puréeing and reheating.

2 Stir the peas into the pan, add the stock and mint and bring to a boil. Cover and simmer very gently for about 30 minutes for fresh peas, or 15 minutes if you are using frozen peas, until the peas are very tender. Remove about 3 tablespoons of the peas, using a slotted spoon, and put to one side for the garnish.

3 Pour the soup into a food processor or blender, add the milk and purée until smooth. Then return the soup to the pan and reheat gently. Season to taste, adding a pinch of sugar, if liked.

4 Pour the soup into individual bowls. Swirl a little cream into each, then garnish with mint and the reserved peas.

Carrot and Coriander Soup

Use a good homemade stock for this soup – it adds a far greater depth of flavor than stock made from cubes.

INGREDIENTS

Serves 4

4 tablespoons butter

3 leeks, sliced

1 pound carrots, sliced

1 tablespoon ground coriander

5 cups homemade/canned chicken stock

2/3 cup plain yogurt,
   preferably sheep's milk

salt and black pepper

2–3 tablespoons chopped cilantro,
   to garnish

1 Melt the butter in a large pan. Add the leeks and carrots and stir well to coat with the butter. Cover and cook for about 10 minutes, until the vegetables are beginning to soften but not color.

2 Stir in the ground coriander and cook for about 1 minute. Pour in the stock and season to taste. Bring to a boil, cover, and simmer for about 20 minutes, until the leeks and carrots are tender.

3 Let cool slightly, then puree the soup in a blender until smooth. Return the soup to the pan and add 2 tablespoons of the yogurt, then taste the soup and adjust the seasoning. Reheat gently but do not boil.

4 Ladle the soup into bowls and add a spoonful of yogurt to the center of each. Sprinkle on the cilantro and serve immediately.

Leek, Potato and Arugula Soup

Arugula, with its distinctive, peppery taste, is wonderful in this deliciously filling soup. Serve it hot with Italian bread croutons.

INGREDIENTS

Serves 4–6

4 tablespoons butter

1 onion, chopped

3 leeks, chopped

2 potatoes, diced

$3^3/4$ cups light homemade or canned
   chicken stock

2 large handfuls arugula,
   coarsely chopped

$2/3$ cup heavy cream

salt and black pepper

garlic-flavored croutons, to serve

1 Melt the butter in a large heavy-bottomed pan, add the onion, leeks and potatoes and stir until the vegetables are coated.

2 Cover and let the vegetables sweat for about 15 minutes. Pour in the stock, cover once again, then simmer the vegetables for 20 minutes, until tender.

3 Press the soup through a sieve or food mill and return to the rinsed-out pan. (When puréeing the soup, don't use a blender or food processor, as these will give the soup a gluey texture.) Add the chopped arugula and cook gently for 5 minutes.

4 Stir in the cream, then season to taste and reheat gently. Ladle the soup into warm soup bowls and serve with the garlic-flavored croutons.

Split Pea and Zucchini Soup

Rich and satisfying, this tasty and nutritious soup will warm you up on a chilly winter's day.

INGREDIENTS

Serves 4

1 cup yellow split peas
1 medium onion, finely chopped
1 teaspoon sunflower oil
2 medium zucchini, finely diced
4 cups homemade/canned chicken stock
$^{1}/_{2}$ teaspoon ground turmeric
salt and black pepper

3 Reserve a handful of zucchini and add the rest to the pan. Cook, stirring, for 2–3 minutes. Add the stock and turmeric and bring to a boil. Reduce the heat, cover and simmer for 30–40 minutes, until the peas are tender.

4 When the soup is almost ready, bring a saucepan of water to a boil, add the reserved diced zucchini and cook for 1 minute, then drain and add to the soup. Adjust the seasoning to taste.

1 Place the split peas in a bowl, cover with cold water and let soak for several hours or overnight. Drain, rinse in cold water and drain again.

2 Cook the onion in the oil in a covered pan, shaking occasionally, until soft.

COOK'S TIP

For a quicker alternative, use split red lentils for this soup – they need no presoaking and cook very quickly. Adjust the amount of stock, if necessary.

Red Bell Pepper Soup with Lime

The beautiful rich red color of this soup makes it a very attractive first course or light lunch. For a special dinner, toast some tiny croutons and serve sprinkled on the soup.

Serves 4–6

4 red bell peppers, seeded and chopped

1 large onion, chopped

1 teaspoon olive oil

1 garlic clove, crushed

1 small red chili, sliced

3 tablespoons tomato paste

3³/4 cups homemade or canned chicken stock

finely grated rind and juice of 1 lime

salt and black pepper

shreds of lime rind, to garnish

1 Cook the chopped peppers and onion gently in the oil in a covered saucepan for about 5 minutes or until softened, shaking the pan occasionally.

2 Stir in the garlic, then add the chili with the tomato paste. Stir in half the stock, then bring to a boil. Cover the pan and simmer for 10 minutes.

3 Cool slightly, then purée in a food processor or blender. Return to the pan, then add the remaining stock, the lime rind and juice, and seasoning.

4 Bring the soup back to a boil, then serve at once with a few strips of lime rind sprinkled into each bowl.

Jerusalem Artichoke Soup

Topped with saffron cream, this soup is wonderful on a wintry day.

INGREDIENTS

Serves 4

4 tablespoons butter

1 onion, chopped

1 pound Jerusalem artichokes,
   peeled and cut into chunks

3¾ cups homemade or canned
   chicken stock

⅔ cup milk

⅔ cup heavy cream

good pinch of saffron powder

salt and black pepper

chopped fresh chives, to garnish

1 Melt the butter in a large heavy-bottomed pan and cook the chopped onion for about 5–8 minutes, until soft but not browned, stirring occasionally.

2 Add the artichokes to the pan and stir until coated in the butter. Cover and cook gently for 10–15 minutes; do not allow the artichokes to brown. Pour in the stock and milk, then cover and simmer for 15 minutes. Cool slightly, then process in a blender or food processor until smooth.

3 Strain the soup back into the pan. Add half the cream, season to taste and reheat gently. Lightly whip the remaining cream with the saffron powder. Ladle the soup into warmed soup bowls and put a spoonful of saffron cream in the center of each. Sprinkle with chopped chives and serve at once.

Broccoli and Stilton Soup

A really easy, but rich, soup – choose something simple to follow, such as plainly roasted or broiled meat, poultry or fish.

INGREDIENTS

Serves 4

12 ounces broccoli

2 tablespoons butter

1 onion, chopped

1 leek, white part only, chopped

1 small potato, cut into chunks

2½ cups homemade or canned
   hot chicken stock

1¼ cups milk

3 tablespoons heavy cream

4 ounces Stilton cheese, no rind, crumbled

salt and black pepper

1 Break the broccoli into florets, discarding any tough stems. Set aside two small, well-shaped florets to use for the garnish

2 Melt the butter in a large pan and cook the onion and leek until soft but not colored. Add the broccoli and potato, then pour in the stock. Cover and simmer for 15–20 minutes, until tender.

3 Cool slightly, then purée the soup in a blender or food processor. Strain through a sieve back into the pan.

4 Add the milk, cream and seasoning to the pan and reheat gently. At the last minute add the cheese, stirring until it just melts. Do not boil.

5 Meanwhile, blanch the reserved broccoli florets and cut them vertically into thin slices. Ladle the soup into warm bowls and garnish with the broccoli and freshly ground black pepper.

Beet and Apricot Swirl

This soup is most attractive if you swirl together the two colored mixtures, but if you prefer, they can be mixed together to save on time and clean-up.

INGREDIENTS

Serves 4

4 large cooked beets, coarsely
   chopped
1 small onion, coarsely chopped
2¹/₂ cups homemade or canned
   chicken stock
1 cup dried apricots
1 cup orange juice
salt and black pepper

1 Place the beets and half the onion in a pan with the stock. Bring to a boil, then reduce the heat, cover, and simmer for about 10 minutes. Purée in a food processor or blender.

2 Place the rest of the onion in a saucepan with the apricots and orange juice, cover, and simmer gently for about 15 minutes, until tender. Process to a purée in a food processor or blender.

3 Return the two mixtures to the saucepans and reheat. Season to taste with salt and pepper, then swirl them together in individual soup bowls for a marbled effect.

COOK'S TIP

The apricot mixture should be the same consistency as the beet mixture – if it is too thick, then add a little more orange juice.

Spicy Corn Soup

If you are using frozen shrimp, then defrost them before adding them to the soup.

INGREDIENTS

Serves 4

$1/2$ teaspoon sesame or sunflower oil

2 scallions, thinly sliced

1 garlic clove, crushed

$2^1/2$ cups homemade or canned
   chicken stock

15-ounce can cream-style corn

$1^1/4$ cups cooked, peeled shrimp

1 teaspoon green chili paste or
   chili sauce (optional)

salt and black pepper

cilantro leaves, to garnish

1 Heat the oil in a large heavy-bottomed saucepan and sauté the scallions and garlic over medium heat for 1 minute, until softened, but not browned.

COOK'S TIP

If cream-style corn is not available, use ordinary canned corn, puréed in a food processor for just a few seconds, until creamy yet with some texture left.

2 Stir in the chicken stock, cream-style corn, shrimp and chili paste or sauce, if using.

3 Bring the soup to a boil, stirring occasionally. Season to taste, then serve at once, sprinkled with cilantro leaves.

Chicken Goujons

Serve as a first course for eight people or as a filling main course for four. Delicious served with baby new potatoes and a green salad.

INGREDIENTS

Serves 8

4 boned and skinned chicken breasts
3 cups fresh breadcrumbs
1 teaspoon ground coriander
2 teaspoons ground paprika
$1/2$ teaspoon ground cumin
3 tablespoons all-purpose flour
2 eggs, beaten
oil, for deep-frying
salt and black pepper
lemon slices, to garnish
sprigs of cilantro, to garnish

For the dip
$1^1/4$ cups strained plain yogurt
2 tablespoons lemon juice
4 tablespoons chopped cilantro
4 tablespoons chopped fresh parsley

1 Divide each chicken breast into two natural fillets. Place them between two sheets of plastic wrap and using a rolling pin, flatten each one to a thickness of $1/2$ inch.

2 Cut the chicken into diagonal 1-in strips.

3 Mix the breadcrumbs with the spices and seasoning. Toss the chicken fillet pieces (goujons) in the flour, keeping them separate.

4 Dip the goujons into the beaten egg and then coat with the breadcrumb mixture.

5 Thoroughly combine all the ingredients for the dip and season to taste. Cover and chill until needed.

6 Heat the oil in a heavy-bottomed pan. It is ready for deep-frying when a piece of bread tossed into the oil sizzles on the surface. Fry the goujons in batches until golden and crisp. Drain on paper towels and keep warm in the oven until all the chicken has been fried. Garnish with lemon slices and sprigs of cilantro and serve with the yogurt dip.

Corn-fed Chicken Salad

A light first course for eight or a substantial main course for four.

INGREDIENTS

Serves 8

4 pounds corn-fed or free range chicken

1¹/4 cups white wine and water, mixed

¹/4-inch slices French bread

1 garlic clove, peeled

8 ounces green beans, trimmed and cut in
    2-inch lengths

4 ounces fresh young spinach leaves,
    washed and torn into small pieces

2 celery stalks, thinly sliced

2 sun-dried tomatoes, chopped

2 scallions, thinly sliced

fresh chives and parsley, to garnish

For the vinaigrette

2 tablespoons red wine vinegar

6 tablespoons olive oil

1 tablespoon whole-grain mustard

1 tablespoon honey

2 tablespoons chopped mixed fresh herbs

2 teaspoons finely chopped capers

salt and black pepper

2 Put all the ingredients for the vinaigrette into a screw-top jar and shake vigorously. Adjust the seasoning to taste.

3 Toast the French bread until golden brown. Rub with garlic.

4 Cook the green beans in boiling water until just tender. Drain and rinse under cold water.

5 Arrange the spinach on serving plates with the sliced celery, green beans, sun-dried tomatoes, chicken and scallions. Spoon on the dressing, arrange the toasted croutes and garnish with fresh chives and parsley.

1 Preheat the oven to 375°F. Put the chicken, wine and water into a casserole. Roast for 1¹/2 hours, until tender. Let cool in the liquid. Remove the skin and bones and cut the flesh into small pieces.

Chicken Liver Pâté

*A deliciously smooth pâté which is
ideal to spread on hot toast.*

Serves 6 or more

4 tablespoons butter
1 onion, finely chopped
12 ounces chicken livers, trimmed of all
    dark or greenish parts
4 tablespoons medium sherry
1 ounce cream cheese
1–2 tablespoons lemon juice
2 hard-boiled eggs, chopped
salt and pepper
1/4 cup clarified butter

1 Melt the butter in a frying pan.
Add the onion and livers and
cook until the onion is soft and the
livers are lightly browned and no
longer pink in the center.

2 Add the sherry and boil until
reduced by half. Cool slightly.

COOK'S TIP

Add brandy instead of sherry for
a special occasion dinner party.

3 Turn the mixture into a food
processor or blender and add
the cream cheese and 1 tablespoon
lemon juice. Blend until smooth.

4 Add the hard-boiled eggs and
blend briefly. Season with salt
and pepper. Taste and add more
lemon juice, if desired.

5 Pack the liver pâté into a mold
or into individual ramekins.
Smooth the surface.

6 Spoon a layer of clarified
butter over the surface of the
pâté. Chill until firm. Serve at
room temperature, with hot toast
or crackers.

Chicken and Avocado Mayonnaise

You need really firm scoops or forks to eat this appetizer, so don't be tempted to try to pass it around as a finger food.

INGREDIENTS

Serves 4

2 tablespoons mayonnaise

1 tablespoon ricotta or farmer's cheese

2 garlic cloves, crushed

1 cup chopped cooked chicken

1 large ripe, but firm, avocado,
    peeled and pitted

2 tablespoons lemon juice

salt and black pepper

corn chips or tortilla chips, to serve

1 Mix together the mayonnaise, ricotta, garlic, and seasoning to taste, in a small bowl. Stir in the chopped chicken.

COOK'S TIP
~

This mixture also makes a great, chunky filling for sandwiches, rolls or pita bread. Or, serve as a main course salad, heaped onto a base of mixed salad leaves.

2 Chop the avocado and toss immediately in lemon juice.

3 Mix the avocado gently into the chicken mixture. Check the seasoning and chill until needed.

4 Serve in small serving dishes with the corn or tortilla chips as scoops, if desired.

Nutty Chicken Balls

Serve these as a first course with the lemon sauce, or make them into smaller balls and serve on toothpicks as canapés.

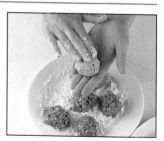

1 tablespoon lemon juice
1 tablespoon chopped fresh parsley
1 tablespoon chopped fresh chives

INGREDIENTS

Serves 4
12 ounces chicken
$^1/_2$ cup pistachios, finely
   chopped
1 tablespoon lemon juice
2 eggs, beaten
all-purpose flour, for shaping
$1^1/_4$ cups blanched chopped
   almonds
$^3/_4$ cup dried breadcrumbs
salt and black pepper

For the lemon sauce
$^2/_3$ cup homemade or canned
   chicken stock
1 cup cream cheese

1 Skin and grind or chop the chicken finely. Mix with salt and freshly ground black pepper, pistachios, lemon juice and one beaten egg.

2 Shape into sixteen small balls with floured hands (use a spoon as a guide, so that all the balls are roughly the same size). Roll the balls in the remaining beaten egg and coat first with the almonds and then the dried breadcrumbs, pressing on firmly. Chill until ready to cook.

3 Preheat the oven to 375°F. Place the balls on a greased baking sheet and bake for about 15 minutes, or until golden brown and crisp.

4 To make the lemon sauce, gently heat the chicken stock and cream cheese together in a pan, whisking until smooth. Add the lemon juice, herbs and seasoning. Serve with the chicken balls.

Spiced Chicken Livers

Chicken livers can be bought frozen, but make sure that you defrost them thoroughly before using. Serve as a first course or light meal along with a mixed salad and garlic bread.

INGREDIENTS

Serves 4

12 ounces chicken livers

1 cup all-purpose flour

$^1/_2$ teaspoon ground coriander

$^1/_2$ teaspoon ground cumin

$^1/_2$ teaspoon ground cardamom
    seeds

$^1/_4$ teaspoon ground paprika

$^1/_4$ teaspoon ground nutmeg

6 tablespoons olive oil

salt and black pepper

1 Dry the chicken livers on paper towels, removing any unwanted pieces. Cut the large livers in half and leave the smaller ones whole.

2 Mix the flour with all the spices and the seasoning.

3 Coat a few of the livers with spiced flour, separating each piece. Heat the oil in a large frying pan and fry the livers in small batches. (This helps to keep the oil temperature high and prevents the flour from becoming soggy.)

4 Fry quickly, stirring frequently, until crisp. Keep warm, and repeat with the remaining livers. Serve immediately with warm garlic bread and salad.

Mediterranean Tomato Soup

*Children will love this soup –
especially if you use fancy pasta
shapes such as alphabet letters
or animals.*

Serves 4

1¹/₂ pounds ripe plum tomatoes
1 medium onion, quartered
1 celery stalk
1 garlic clove
1 tablespoon olive oil
2 cups homemade or canned
   chicken stock
1 tablespoon tomato paste
¹/₂ cup small pasta shapes
salt and black pepper
cilantro or parsley, to garnish

1 Put the tomatoes, onion, celery
and garlic in a pan with the oil.
Cover and cook over low heat for
40–45 minutes, shaking the pan
occasionally, until very soft.

2 Spoon the vegetables into a
food processor or blender and
process until smooth. Press
through a sieve back into the pan.

3 Stir in the stock and tomato
paste and bring to a boil. Add
the pasta and simmer gently for
about 8 minutes, or until the pasta
is tender. Add salt and pepper to
taste, then sprinkle with cilantro or
parsley and serve hot.

Mushroom, Celery and Garlic Soup

*Worcestershire sauce makes this
mushroom soup extra tasty.*

Serves 4

4¹/₂ cups chopped mushrooms
4 celery stalks, chopped
3 garlic cloves
3 tablespoons dry sherry or white wine
3 cups homemade or canned
   chicken stock
2 tablespoons Worcestershire sauce
1 teaspoon grated nutmeg
salt and black pepper
celery leaves, to garnish

1 Place the mushrooms, celery
and garlic in a pan and stir in
the sherry or wine. Cover and cook
over low heat for about 30–40
minutes, until tender.

3 Bring to a boil, season to taste
and serve hot, garnished with
celery leaves.

2 Add half the stock and purée in
a food processor or blender,
until smooth. Return to the pan
and add the remaining stock, the
Worcestershire sauce and nutmeg,

Chicken Liver and Marsala Pâté

This is a really quick and simple pâté, yet it has a delicious – and quite sophisticated – flavor. It contains Marsala, a soft and pungent fortified wine from Sicily. If it is unavailable, use brandy or a medium-dry sherry.

INGREDIENTS

Serves 4

12 ounces chicken livers,
    defrosted if frozen
1 cup butter, softened
2 garlic cloves, crushed
1 tablespoon Marsala
1 teaspoon chopped fresh sage
salt and black pepper
8 sage leaves, to garnish
thin, crisp toast, to serve

1 Pick over the chicken livers, then rinse and dry with paper towels. Melt 2 tablespoons of the butter in a frying pan, and fry the chicken livers with the garlic over medium heat for about 5 minutes, or until they are firm but still pink in the middle.

2 Transfer the livers to a blender or food processor, using a slotted spoon, and add the Marsala and chopped sage.

3 Melt 10 tablespoons of the remaining butter in the frying pan, stirring to loosen any residue, then pour into the blender or processor and blend until smooth. Season well.

4 Spoon the pâté into four individual pots and smooth the surface. Melt the remaining butter in a separate pan and pour over the pâtés. Garnish with sage leaves and chill until set. Serve with triangles of toast.

Smoked Chicken and Lentil Soup

Smoked chicken gives added depth of flavor to this hearty soup.

INGREDIENTS

Serves 4

2 tablespoons butter

1 large carrot, chopped

1 onion, chopped

1 celery stalk, chopped

1 leek, white part only, chopped

1^1/$_2$ cups mushrooms, chopped

^{1}/$_4$ cup dry white wine

4 cups homemade or canned
   chicken stock

2 teaspoons dried thyme

1 bay leaf

^{1}/$_2$ cup lentils

1^1/$_2$ cups smoked chicken meat, diced

salt and pepper

chopped fresh parsley, to garnish

1 Melt the butter in a large saucepan. Add the carrot, onion, celery, leek and mushrooms. Cook gently until golden, about 3–5 minutes.

2 Stir in the wine and chicken stock. Bring to a boil and skim any foam that rises to the surface. Add the thyme and bay leaf. Lower the heat, cover, and simmer gently for 30 minutes.

3 Add the lentils and continue cooking, covered, until they are just tender, 30–40 minutes more. Stir the soup occasionally.

4 Stir in the chicken and season to taste. Cook until just heated through. Ladle into bowls and garnish with chopped parsley.

Chicken Cigars

These small crispy rolls can be served warm as canapés with a drink before a meal, or as a first course with a crisp, colorful salad.

INGREDIENTS

Serves 4

10-ounce package of filo pastry, defrosted
3 tablespoons olive oil
fresh parsley, to garnish

For the filling

3 cups ground raw chicken
salt and freshly ground black pepper
1 egg, beaten
$1/2$ teaspoon ground cinnamon
$1/2$ teaspoon ground ginger
2 tablespoons raisins
1 tablespoon olive oil
1 small onion, finely chopped

1 Mix all the filling ingredients, except the oil and onion, in a bowl. Heat the oil in a large frying pan and cook the onion until tender. Let cool. Add the mixed filling ingredients.

2 Preheat the oven to 350°F. Once the filo pastry package has been opened, keep the pastry covered at all times with a damp dish towel. Work fast, as the filo pastry dries out very quickly when exposed to the air. Unroll the pastry and cut it into 10 x 4 inch strips.

3 Take a strip (cover the remainder), brush with a little oil and place a small spoonful of filling about $1/2$ inch from the end.

4 To encase the filling, fold the sides inward to a width of 2 inches and roll into a cigar shape. Place on a greased baking sheet and brush with oil. Repeat to use all the filling. Bake for about 20–25 minutes, until golden brown and crisp. Garnish with fresh parsley and serve.

Chicken Roulades

These chicken rolls make a light lunch dish for two, or an appetizer for four. They can be sliced and served cold with a salad.

INGREDIENTS

Makes 4

4 chicken thighs, boned and skinned
4 ounces chopped fresh or frozen spinach
1 tablespoon butter
2 tablespoons pine nuts
pinch of grated nutmeg
7 tablespoons fresh white breadcrumbs
4 strips lean bacon
2 tablespoons olive oil
2/3 cup white wine
    or chicken stock
2 teaspoons cornstarch
2 tablespoons light cream
1 tablespoon chopped fresh chives
salt and black pepper

1 Preheat the oven to 350°F. Place the chicken thighs between plastic wrap and flatten with a rolling pin.

2 Put the spinach and butter into a saucepan, heat gently until the spinach has defrosted, if frozen, then increase the heat and cook rapidly, stirring occasionally, until all the moisture has been cooked off. Add the pine nuts, seasoning, nutmeg and fresh breadcrumbs.

3 Divide the filling between the chicken pieces and roll up neatly. Wrap a strip of bacon around each piece and tie securely with fine string.

4 Heat the oil in a large frying pan and brown the rolls all over. Lift out, using a slotted spoon to drain off the oil, and place in a shallow ovenproof dish.

5 Pour on the wine or stock, cover, and bake for 15–20 minutes, or until tender. Transfer the chicken to a serving plate and remove the string. Strain the cooking liquid into a saucepan.

6 Blend the cornstarch with a little cold water and add to the juices in the pan, along with the cream. Bring to a boil, stirring until thick. Adjust the seasoning and add the chives. Pour the sauce around the chicken and serve.

Chicken, Bacon and Walnut Terrine

*To seal the terrine in the pan for
longer storage, pour on melted fat.*

INGREDIENTS

Serves 8–10

2 boneless chicken breasts

1 large garlic clove, crushed

$^{1}/_{2}$ slice bread

1 egg

12 ounces bacon (the fattier the better),
   ground or finely chopped

8 ounces chicken or turkey livers,
   finely chopped

$^{1}/_{4}$ cup chopped walnuts, toasted

2 tablespoons sweet sherry or Madeira

$^{1}/_{2}$ teaspoon ground allspice

$^{1}/_{2}$ teaspoon cayenne pepper

pinch each ground nutmeg and cloves

8 long strips lean bacon,
   rind removed

salt and black pepper

chicory leaves and chives, to garnish

1 Cut the chicken breasts into thin strips and season lightly. Mash the garlic, bread and egg together. Work in the chopped bacon (using your hands is really the best way) and then the finely chopped livers. Stir in the chopped walnuts, sherry or Madeira, spices and seasoning to taste.

2 Preheat the oven to 400°F. Stretch out the bacon and use to line a 1$^{1}/_{2}$-pound loaf pan, then pack in half the meat mixture.

3 Lay the chicken strips on the top and spread the rest of the mixture over. Cover the loaf pan with lightly-greased foil, seal well and press down very firmly.

4 Place the terrine in a roasting pan half-full of hot water and bake for 1–1$^{1}/_{2}$ hours, or until firm to the touch. Remove from the oven, place weights on the top and let cool completely. Drain off any excess fat or liquid while the terrine is warm.

5 When it's really cold, turn out the terrine, cut into thick slices and serve at once, garnished with a few chicory leaves and chives.

Mini Spring Rolls

Use a wok or a large frying pan for this recipe. For a spicier version, sprinkle with a little cayenne pepper.

INGREDIENTS

Makes 20

1 green chili

$^1/_2$ cup vegetable oil

1 small onion, finely chopped

1 clove garlic, crushed

3 ounces cooked chicken breast

1 small carrot, cut into fine matchsticks

1 scallion, finely sliced

1 small red bell pepper, seeded and cut
    into fine matchsticks

1 ounce beansprouts

1 tablespoon sesame oil

4 large sheets filo pastry

egg white, lightly beaten

long chives, to garnish (optional)

3 tablespoons light soy sauce, to serve

1 Carefully remove the seeds from the chili and chop finely, wearing rubber gloves to protect your hands, if necessary.

2 Heat the wok, then add 2 tablespoons of the vegetable oil. When hot, add the onion, garlic and chili. Stir-fry for 1 minute.

3 Slice the chicken thinly, then add to the wok and fry over high heat, stirring and tossing constantly until browned.

4 Add the carrot, scallion and red pepper and stir-fry for 2 minutes. Add the beansprouts, stir in the sesame oil, remove from the heat and let cool.

COOK'S TIP

Always keep filo pastry sheets covered with a damp, clean cloth until needed, to prevent them from drying out.

5 Cut each sheet of filo into 5 short strips. Place a small amount of filling at one end of each strip, then fold in the long sides and roll up the pastry. Seal and glaze the rolls with the egg white, then chill, uncovered, for 15 minutes before frying.

6 Wipe out the wok with paper towels, heat it, and add the remaining vegetable oil. When the oil is hot, fry the rolls in batches, until crisp and golden brown. Drain on paper towels and serve with light soy sauce.

Sesame Seed Chicken Morsels

Stir-fry these crunchy morsels in a wok, then serve them warm with a glass of chilled dry white wine.

INGREDIENTS

Makes 20

6 ounces raw chicken breast
2 cloves garlic, crushed
1-inch piece fresh ginger,
   peeled and grated
1 medium egg white
1 teaspoon cornstarch
$^1/_4$ cup shelled pistachios,
   coarsely chopped
4 tablespoons sesame seeds
2 tablespoons grapeseed oil
salt and black pepper

For the sauce
3 tablespoons hoisin sauce
1 tablespoon sweet chili sauce

To garnish
fresh root ginger, finely shredded
pistachios, coarsely chopped
fresh dill sprigs

1 Place the chicken, garlic, grated ginger, egg white and cornstarch in a food processor or blender and process to a smooth paste.

2 Stir in the pistachios and season with salt and pepper.

3 Roll into 20 balls and coat with sesame seeds. Heat the wok and add the oil. When the oil is hot, stir-fry the chicken in batches, turning regularly until golden. Drain on paper towels.

4 For the sauce, mix together the hoisin and chili sauces in a bowl. Garnish the chicken morsels with shredded ginger, pistachios and dill. Serve hot, with a dish of sauce for dipping.

Spicy Chicken Canapés

These tiny little cocktail sandwiches have a spicy filling and are finished with different toppings. Use square bread so that you can cut out more rounds and have less wastage.

Makes 18

3/4 cup finely chopped cooked
　chicken
2 scallions, finely chopped
2 tablespoons chopped red bell pepper
6 tablespoons Curry Mayonnaise
6 slices white bread
1 tablespoon paprika
1 tablespoon chopped fresh parsley
2 tablespoons chopped salted
　peanuts

2 Spread the mixture over three of the bread slices and sandwich with the remaining bread, pressing well together. Spread the remaining Curry Mayonnaise over the top and cut into 1 1/2-inch circles using a round cutter.

3 Dip into paprika, chopped parsley or chopped nuts and arrange attractively on a plate.

1 In a bowl, mix the chopped chicken with the chopped scallions, red pepper and half the Curry Mayonnaise.

Chicken Roule

*A relatively simple dish to prepare,
this recipe uses ground beef as a
filling. It is rolled in chicken fillet
which is spread with a garlic cheese,
which just melts in the mouth.*

INGREDIENTS

Serves 4

4 boneless chicken breasts,
    about 4 ounces each
1 cup ground beef
2 tablespoons chopped fresh chives
8 ounces Boursin or garlic
    cream cheese
2 tablespoons honey
salt and black pepper

1 Preheat the oven to 375°F.
Place the chicken breasts, side
by side, between two pieces of
plastic wrap. Beat with a meat
mallet until ¹/₂-inch thick and
joined together.

2 Place the ground beef in a large
pan. Fry for 3 minutes, add the
fresh chives and seasoning. Cool.

3 Place the chicken on a board
and spread with the cream
cheese.

4 Top with the beef mixture,
spreading it over evenly.

5 Roll up the chicken tightly to
form a sausage shape.

6 Brush with honey and place in
a roasting pan. Cook for 1 hour
in the preheated oven. Remove
from the pan and slice thinly. Serve
with freshly cooked vegetables.

Chicken with Apricot and Pecan Baskets

The potato baskets make a pretty addition to the chicken and could easily have different fillings, if you feel like for a change.

INGREDIENTS

Serves 8

8 chicken breast fillets

2 tablespoons butter

6 mushrooms, chopped

1 tablespoon chopped pecan nuts

$2/3$ cup chopped, cooked ham

1 cup whole wheat breadcrumbs

1 tablespoon chopped parsley, plus some whole leaves to garnish

salt and pepper

cocktail sticks to secure rolls

Sauce

1 tablespoon cornstarch

$1/2$ cup white wine

4 tablespoons butter

$1/4$ cup apricot chutney

Potato baskets

4 large baking potatoes

6 ounces sausage

8-ounce can apricots in natural juice, drained and quartered

$1/4$ teaspoon cinnamon

$1/2$ teaspoon grated orange rind

2 tablespoons maple syrup

2 tablespoons butter

$1/4$ cup chopped pecan nuts, plus some pecan halves to garnish

1 Preheat the oven to 325°F. Put the chicken between two sheets of waxed paper and flatten with a meat pounder. Melt the butter in a pan and sauté the mushrooms, pecans and ham. Stir in the breadcrumbs, parsley and seasoning. Divide the mixture between the chicken breasts, roll up and secure each one with a cocktail stick. Chill.

2 Put the potatoes in the oven to bake. Mix the cornstarch with a little of the wine to make a smooth paste. Put the remaining wine in a pan and add the paste. Cook, stirring, until smooth. Add the butter and apricot chutney and cook for 5 minutes, stirring constantly.

3 Place the chicken breasts in a shallow ovenproof dish and pour over the sauce. Bake in the oven (at the same temperature) for 20 minutes, basting several times.

4 When the potatoes are cooked, cut them in half and scoop out the inside, leaving a reasonable layer within the shell. Mash the potato and place in a mixing bowl.

5 Fry the sausage and drain off any fat. Add the remaining ingredients and cook for 1 minute. Mix together the sausage and potato and put in the potato shells. Sprinkle the pecan halves over the top, put in the oven with the chicken and bake for 30 minutes.

6 Remove the chicken and drain the sauce into a separate container. Slice the breasts, put on plates and pour the sauce over the top. Serve with the potato baskets and garnish with parsley leaves.

Chicken with Yellow Pepper Sauce

Scallops of chicken filled with garlic cheese with yellow pepper sauce.

INGREDIENTS

Serves 4

2 tablespoons olive oil

2 large yellow bell peppers, seeded and
    chopped

1 small onion, chopped

1 tablespoon fresh squeezed orange juice

1¼ cups homemade/canned chicken
    stock

4 chicken breasts

3 ounces Boursin or garlic cream cheese

12 fresh basil leaves

2 tablespoons butter

salt and black pepper

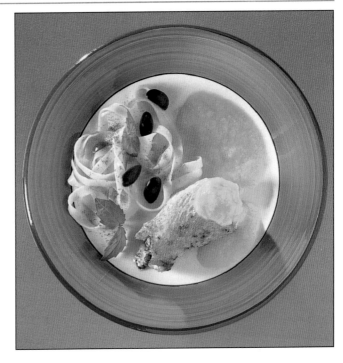

1 To make the yellow pepper
sauce, heat half the oil in a pan
and gently fry the peppers and
onion until beginning to soften.
Add the orange juice and stock and
cook until very soft.

3 Spread the chicken fillets with
the Boursin or garlic cream
cheese. Chop half the basil and
sprinkle on top, then roll up the
fillets, tucking in the ends like an
envelope, and secure neatly with
half a toothpick.

5 While the fillets are cooking,
press the pepper mixture
through a sieve, or blend until
smooth, then strain back into the
pan. Season to taste and warm
through, or serve cold, with the
fillets, garnished with the remaining basil leaves.

2 Meanwhile, lay the chicken
fillets out flat and pound
them lightly.

4 Heat the remaining oil and the
butter in a frying pan and fry
the fillets for 7–8 minutes, turning
them frequently, until golden and
cooked through.

COOK'S TIP
Turkey or veal scallops could be
used in place of the chicken,
if you prefer.

Chili Chicken Couscous

Couscous is a convenient alternative to rice and makes a good base for all kinds of ingredients.

INGREDIENTS

Serves 4

2 cups couscous

4 cups boiling water

1 teaspoon olive oil

14 ounces chicken without
   skin and bone, diced

1 yellow bell pepper, seeded and sliced

2 large zucchini, sliced thickly

1 small green chili, thinly sliced,
   or 1 teaspoon chili sauce

1 large tomato, diced

15-ounce can chickpeas, drained

salt and black pepper

cilantro or parsley sprigs to garnish

1 Place the couscous in a large bowl and pour boiling water over it. Cover and let stand for 30 minutes.

2 Heat the oil in a large, non-stick pan and stir-fry the chicken quickly, then reduce the heat.

3 Stir in the pepper, zucchini and chili or sauce and cook for about 10 minutes, until the vegetables are softened.

4 Stir in the tomato and chick-peas, then add the couscous. Adjust the seasoning and stir over medium heat until hot. Serve garnished with sprigs of fresh cilantro or parsley.

Chicken Bean Bake

Sliced eggplant layered with beans and chicken and topped with yogurt.

INGREDIENTS

Serves 4

1 medium eggplant, thinly sliced

1 tablespoon olive oil, for brushing

1 pound boneless chicken breast, diced

1 medium onion, chopped

14-ounce can chopped tomatoes

15-ounce can red kidney beans, drained

1 tablespoon paprika

1 tablespoon chopped fresh thyme,
   or 1 teaspoon dried

1 teaspoon chili sauce

1 1/2 cups strained plain yogurt

1/2 teaspoon nutmeg

salt and black pepper

1 Preheat the oven to 375°F. Arrange the eggplant in a colander and sprinkle with salt.

2 Set the eggplant aside for 30 minutes, then rinse and pat dry. Brush a nonstick pan with oil and fry the eggplant in batches, turning once, until golden.

3 Remove the eggplant, add the chicken and onion to the pan, and cook until lightly browned.

Stir in the tomatoes, beans, paprika, thyme, chili sauce and seasoning. In a bowl, combine the yogurt and nutmeg.

4 Layer the meat and eggplant in an ovenproof dish, finishing with eggplant. Spread the yogurt

evenly over the top and bake for 50–60 minutes, until golden.

Chicken Spirals

These little spirals look impressive, but they're very simple to make, and a good way to jazz up plain chicken.

INGREDIENTS

Serves 4

4 chicken breasts, about 3¹/₂ ounces
  each, thinly sliced

4 teaspoons tomato paste

¹/₂ cup large basil
  leaves

1 garlic clove, crushed

1 tablespoon skim milk

2 tablespoons whole wheat flour

salt and black pepper

puréed tomatoes or fresh tomato sauce
  and pasta, to serve

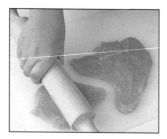

1 Place the chicken breasts on a board. If too thick, flatten them slightly by beating with a rolling pin or meat market.

2 Spread each chicken fillet with tomato paste, then top with a few basil leaves, a little crushed garlic and seasoning.

3 Roll up firmly around the filling and secure with a toothpick. Brush with milk and sprinkle with flour to coat lightly.

4 Place the spirals on a foil-lined broiler pan. Cook them under a medium-hot broiler for 15–20 minutes, turning occasionally, until thoroughly cooked. Serve hot, sliced, with a spoonful or two of puréed tomatoes or sauce and accompanied with pasta sprinkled with fresh basil.

COOK'S TIP

When flattening the chicken fillets with a rolling pin, place them between two sheets of plastic wrap.

Monday Savory Omelet

Use up all your leftover odds and ends in this tasty omelet.

INGREDIENTS

Serves 4–6

2 tablespoons olive oil

1 large onion, chopped

2 large garlic cloves, crushed

4 ounces rindless bacon, chopped

2 ounces cold cooked chicken, chopped

4 ounces leftover cooked vegetables
(preferably ones which are not too soft)

1 cup leftover cooked rice or pasta

4 eggs

2 tablespoons chopped, mixed fresh
herbs, such as parsley, chives, marjoram
or tarragon, or 2 teaspoons dried

1 teaspoon Worcestershire sauce,
or more to taste

1 tablespoon grated aged
Cheddar cheese

salt and black pepper

1 Heat the oil in a large flame-proof frying pan and sauté the onion, garlic and bacon until all the fat has run out of the bacon.

2 Add the chopped chicken, vegetables and rice (or pasta). Beat the eggs, herbs and Worcestershire sauce together with seasoning. Pour over the rice (or pasta) and vegetables, stir lightly, then leave the mixture undisturbed to cook gently for about 5 minutes.

3 When just beginning to set, sprinkle with the cheese and place under a preheated broiler until just firm and golden.

COOK'S TIP

This is surprisingly good cold, so it's perfect for taking on picnics, or using for packed lunches.

Chicken Lasagne

Based on the Italian beef lasagne, this is an excellent dish for entertaining guests of all ages. Serve simply with a green salad.

Serves 8

2 tablespoons olive oil

2 pounds ground chicken

1¹/₂ cups rindless lean bacon strips, chopped

2 garlic cloves, crushed

1 pound leeks, sliced

1¹/₄ cups carrots, diced

2 tablespoons tomato paste

2 cups homemade/canned chicken stock

12 sheets (no need to pre-cook) green lasagne

For the cheese sauce

4 tablespoons butter

¹/₂ cup all-purpose flour

2¹/₂ cups milk

1 cup grated aged Cheddar cheese

¹/₄ teaspoon dry English mustard

salt and black pepper

1 Heat the oil in a large flame-proof casserole and brown the ground chicken and bacon briskly, separating the pieces with a wooden spoon. Add the crushed garlic cloves, sliced leeks and diced carrots and cook for about 5 minutes until softened. Add the tomato paste, stock and seasoning. Bring to a boil, cover and simmer for 30 minutes.

2 To make the sauce, melt the butter in a saucepan, add the flour and gradually blend in the milk, stirring until smooth. Bring to a boil, stirring all the time, until thickened and simmer for several minutes. Add half the grated cheese and the mustard, and season to taste.

3 Preheat the oven to 375°F. Layer the chicken mixture, lasagne and half the cheese sauce in a 10-cup ovenproof dish, starting and finishing with a layer of chicken.

4 Pour the remaining half of the cheese sauce over the top to cover, sprinkle on the remaining cheese and bake in the preheated oven for 1 hour, or until bubbling and lightly browned on top.

Crunchy Stuffed Chicken Breasts

These can be prepared ahead of time as long as the stuffing is entirely cold before the chicken is stuffed. It is an ideal dish for entertaining.

INGREDIENTS

Serves 4

4 chicken breasts, boned
2 tablespoons butter
1 garlic clove, crushed
1 tablespoon Dijon mustard

For the stuffing
1 tablespoon butter
1 bunch scallions, sliced
3 tablespoons fresh breadcrumbs
2 tablespoons pine nuts
1 egg yolk
1 tablespoon chopped fresh parsley
salt and black pepper
4 tablespoons grated cheese

For the topping
2 bacon slices, finely chopped
1 cup fresh breadcrumbs
1 tablespoon grated Parmesan cheese
1 tablespoon chopped fresh parsley

1 Preheat the oven to 400°F. To make the stuffing, heat 1 tablespoon of the butter in a frying pan and cook the scallions until soft. Remove from the heat and allow to cool for a few minutes.

2 Add the remaining ingredients and mix thoroughly.

3 To make the topping, fry the chopped bacon until crisp, drain and add to the breadcrumbs, Parmesan cheese and fresh parsley.

4 Carefully cut a deep pocket in each of the chicken breasts, using a sharp knife.

5 Divide the stuffing into fourths and use to fill the pockets. Put in a buttered ovenproof dish.

6 Melt the remaining butter, mix it with the crushed garlic and mustard, and brush liberally over the chicken. Press on the topping and bake uncovered for about 30–40 minutes, or until tender.

Chicken with Honey and Grapefruit

Chicken breast portions cook very quickly and are ideal for suppers "on-the-run" – but don't be tempted to overcook them. You could substitute boneless turkey breasts, or duck breast fillets for the chicken, if you like.

INGREDIENTS

Serves 4

4 chicken breast portions, skinned

3–4 tablespoons honey

1 pink grapefruit, skinned and
    cut into 12 segments

salt and black pepper

noodles and salad leaves, to serve

1 Make three quite deep, diagonal slits in the chicken flesh, using a large sharp knife.

2 Brush the chicken all over with the honey and sprinkle well with seasoning.

3 Put the chicken in a flameproof dish, the uncut side facing up, and place under a medium broiler for 2–3 minutes.

4 Turn the chicken over and place the grapefruit segments in the slits. Brush with more honey and cook for another 5 minutes, or until tender. If necessary, reduce the heat so that the honey glaze does not burn. Serve at once with noodles and salad leaves.

Crispy Chicken with Garlic Rice

Chicken wings cooked until they are really tender have a surprising amount of meat on them, and make a very economical supper for a crowd of kids – provide lots of paper towels, napkins and finger bowls for the greasy fingers.

INGREDIENTS

Serves 4

1 large onion, chopped

2 garlic cloves, crushed

2 tablespoons sunflower oil

1 1/4 cups basmati rice

1 1/2 cups homemade or canned
    hot chicken stock

2 teaspoons finely grated lemon rind

2 tablespoons chopped mixed herbs

8 or 12 chicken wings

1/2 cup all-purpose flour

salt and black pepper

fresh tomato sauce and
    vegetables, to serve

1 Preheat the oven to 400°F. Fry the onion and garlic in the oil in a large flameproof casserole, until golden. Stir in the rice and toss until all the grains are well coated in oil.

2 Stir in the stock, lemon rind and herbs and bring to a boil. Cover and cook in the middle of the oven for 40–50 minutes. Stir once or twice during cooking.

3 Meanwhile, wipe the chicken wings dry. Season the flour and use to coat the chicken portions thoroughly.

4 Put the chicken wings in a small roasting pan and cook in the top of the oven for 30–40 minutes, turning once, until crisp.

5 Serve the rice and chicken wings with a fresh tomato sauce and a selection of vegetables.

Thai Chicken and Vegetable Stir-fry

Make this easy-to-fix dish a little hotter by adding more fresh ginger.

INGREDIENTS

Serves 4

1 piece lemon grass (or the rind of
   $^{1}/_{2}$ lemon)
$^{1}/_{2}$ in piece of fresh ginger
1 large garlic clove
2 tablespoons sunflower oil
10 ounces lean chicken, thinly sliced
$^{1}/_{2}$ red bell pepper, seeded and sliced
$^{1}/_{2}$ green bell pepper, seeded and sliced
4 scallions, chopped
2 medium carrots, cut into matchsticks
4 ounces thin green beans
2 tablespoons oyster sauce
pinch sugar
salt and black pepper
$^{1}/_{4}$ cup salted peanuts,
   lightly crushed, and cilantro
   leaves, to garnish
cooked rice, to serve

1 Thinly slice the lemon grass or lemon rind. Peel and chop the ginger and garlic. Heat the oil in a frying pan over a high heat. Add the lemon grass or lemon rind, ginger and garlic, and stir-fry for 30 seconds, or until brown.

2 Add the chicken and stir-fry for 2 minutes. Then add the vegetables and stir-fry for 4–5 minutes, until the chicken is cooked and the vegetables are almost cooked.

3 Finally stir in the oyster sauce, sugar and seasoning to taste and stir-fry for another minute to mix well. Serve immediately, sprinkled with the peanuts and cilantro leaves and accompanied with rice.

Chicken with Herbs and Lentils

*Chicken baked on lentils and served
topped with garlic butter.*

INGREDIENTS

Serves 4

4-ounce piece of thick bacon, rind
 removed, chopped

1 large onion, sliced

2 cups well-flavored homemade or canned
 chicken stock

bay leaf

2 sprigs each parsley, marjoram
 and thyme

1 cup green or brown lentils

4 chicken portions

salt and black pepper

2–4 tablespoons garlic butter

COOK'S TIP

For economy's sake buy a
smallish chicken and cut
it in quarters, to give
generous portions.

1 Fry the bacon gently in a large,
heavy-bottomed flameproof
casserole until all the fat runs out
and the bacon begins to brown.
Add the onion and fry for about
another 2 minutes.

2 Stir in the chicken stock, bay
leaf, herb stalks and some of
the leafy parts (keep some herb
sprigs for garnish), lentils and seasoning. Preheat the oven to 375°F.

3 Fry the chicken portions in a
frying pan to brown the skin
before placing on top of the lentils.
Sprinkle with seasoning and some
of the herbs.

4 Cover the casserole and cook
in the oven for about 40
minutes. Serve with a knob of
garlic butter on each portion and a
few of the remaining herb sprigs.

Minty Yogurt Chicken

Chicken marinated with yogurt,
mint, lemon and honey and broiled.

Serves 4

8 chicken thigh portions, skinned
1 tablespoon honey
2 tablespoons lemon (or lime) juice
2 tablespoons plain yogurt
4 tablespoons chopped fresh mint
salt and black pepper
new potatoes and a tomato salad,
   to serve

1 Slash the chicken flesh at regular intervals with a sharp knife. Place in a bowl.

2 Mix together the honey, lime or lemon juice, yogurt, seasoning and half the mint.

3 Spoon the marinade over the chicken and let marinate for 30 minutes. Line the broiler pan with foil and cook the chicken under a medium-hot broiler until thoroughly cooked and golden brown, turning the chicken occasionally during cooking.

4 Sprinkle with the remaining mint and serve with the potatoes and tomato salad.

Oat-crusted Chicken with Sage

Oats make a good coating for savory foods, and here they offer a tasty way to add extra fiber.

INGREDIENTS

Serves 4

3 tablespoons skim milk

2 teaspoons English mustard

$1/2$ cup rolled oats

3 tablespoons chopped sage leaves

8 chicken thighs or drumsticks, skinned

$1/2$ cup low-fat cream or farmer's cheese

1 teaspoon whole-grain mustard

salt and black pepper

fresh sage leaves, to garnish

COOK'S TIP

If fresh sage is not available, choose another fresh herb, such as thyme or parsley, rather than a dried alternative.

1 Preheat the oven to 400°F. Mix together the milk and English mustard.

2 Mix the oats with 2 tablespoons of the sage and the seasoning on a plate. Brush the chicken with the milk and roll it in the oats.

3 Place the chicken on a baking sheet and bake for about 40 minutes, or until the juices run clear, not pink, when pierced through the thickest part.

4 Meanwhile, combine the low-fat cheese, whole-grain mustard, remaining sage and seasoning, then serve with the chicken. Garnish the chicken with fresh sage and serve hot or cold.

Tagine of Chicken

*Based on a traditional Moroccan
dish. The chicken and couscous can
be cooked the day before and
reheated for serving.*

INGREDIENTS

Serves 8

8 chicken legs (thighs and drumsticks)
2 tablespoons olive oil
1 medium onion, finely chopped
2 garlic cloves, crushed
1 teaspoon ground turmeric
$1/2$ teaspoon ground ginger
$1/2$ teaspoon ground cinnamon
2 cups homemade/canned chicken stock
$1^1/4$ cups pitted green olives
1 lemon, sliced
salt and black pepper
cilantro sprigs, to garnish

For the vegetable couscous
$2^1/2$ cups homemade or canned
   chicken stock
1 pound couscous
4 zucchini, thickly sliced
2 carrots, thickly sliced
2 small turnips, peeled and cubed
3 tablespoons olive oil
1 pound can chickpeas, drained
1 tablespoon chopped cilantro

1 Preheat the oven to 350°F. Cut
the chicken legs into two
through the joint.

2 Heat the oil in a large flameproof casserole and brown the
chicken on both sides. Drain,
remove to a dish and keep warm.

3 Add the onion and crushed
garlic to the flameproof
casserole and cook gently until
tender. Add the spices and cook
for 1 minute. Pour on the stock,
bring to a boil, and return the
chicken to the pan. Cover and bake
for 45 minutes, until tender.
Transfer the chicken to a dish,
cover and keep warm.

4 Remove any fat from the
cooking liquid and boil to
reduce by one-third. Meanwhile,
blanch the olives and lemon slices
in a pan of boiling water for 2
minutes, until the lemon skin is
tender. Drain and add to the
cooking liquid, adjusting the
seasoning to taste.

5 To cook the couscous, bring
the stock to a boil in a large
pan and sprinkle in the couscous
slowly, stirring all the time.
Remove from the heat, cover
and let stand for 5 minutes.

6 Meanwhile, cook the prepared
vegetables, drain, and put
them into a large bowl. Add the
couscous and oil and season. Stir
the grains to fluff them up, add the
chickpeas and finally the chopped
cilantro. Spoon onto a large
serving plate, cover with the
chicken, and spoon on the liquid.
Garnish with the cilantro.

Chicken with Asparagus

Canned asparagus may be used instead of fresh, but will not require any cooking – simply add at the very end to warm through.

INGREDIENTS

Serves 4

4 large chicken breasts, boned and
    skinned
1 tablespoon ground cilantro
2 tablespoons olive oil
20 slender asparagus spears, cut
    into 3–4-inch lengths
1^1/4 cups homemade or canned
    chicken stock
1 tablespoon cornstarch
1 tablespoon lemon juice
salt and black pepper
1 tablespoon chopped fresh parsley

1 Split the chicken breasts into two natural fillets. Place each between two sheets of plastic wrap and flatten to a ^{1}/4 inch thickness with a rolling pin. Cut into 1-inch diagonal strips. Sprinkle with cilantro and toss to coat.

2 Heat the oil in a large frying pan and fry the chicken very quickly in small batches for 3–4 minutes, until lightly colored. Season each batch with a little salt and freshly ground black pepper. Remove and keep warm while frying the rest of the chicken.

3 Add the asparagus and chicken stock to the pan and bring to a boil. Cook for another 4–5 minutes, or until tender.

4 Mix the cornstarch to a paste with a little cold water and stir into the sauce to thicken. Return the chicken to the pan and add the lemon juice. Reheat and then serve immediately, garnished with fresh parsley.

Chicken, Carrot and Leek Packages

These intriguing packages may sound fussy for everyday, but they take very little time to make and you can freeze them – ready to cook when defrosted.

INGREDIENTS

Serves 4

4 chicken fillets or boneless breasts

2 small leeks, sliced

2 carrots, grated

4 pitted black olives, chopped

1 garlic clove, crushed

1–2 tablespoons olive oil

8 anchovy fillets

salt and black pepper

black olives and herb sprigs, to garnish

1 Preheat the oven to 400°F. Season the chicken well with salt and pepper.

2 Divide the leeks equally among four sheets of greased waxed paper, about 9 inches square. Place a piece of chicken on top of each one.

3 Mix the carrots, olives, garlic and oil together. Season lightly and place on top of the chicken portions. Top each with two of the anchovy fillets, then carefully wrap up each package, making sure the paper folds are underneath and the carrot mixture on top.

4 Bake for 20 minutes and serve hot, in the paper, garnished with black olives and herb sprigs.

Chicken in a Tomato Coat

Chicken roasted with a coating of tomato sauce and fresh tomatoes.

INGREDIENTS

Serves 4–6

whole free-range chicken,
   3–4¹/₂ pounds

1 small onion

pat of butter

5 tablespoons homemade or canned
   tomato sauce

2 tablespoons chopped, mixed fresh
   herbs, such as parsley, tarragon,
   sage, basil and marjoram, or
   2 teaspoons dried

small glass of dry white wine

2–3 small tomatoes, sliced

olive oil

a little cornstarch (optional)

salt and black pepper

1 Preheat the oven to 375°F. Place the chicken in a roasting pan. Place the onion, the pat of butter and some seasoning inside the chicken.

2 Spread most of the tomato sauce over the chicken and sprinkle with half the herbs and some seasoning. Pour the wine into the roasting pan.

3 Cover with foil, then roast for 1¹/₂ hours, basting occasionally. Remove the foil, spread with the remaining sauce and the sliced tomatoes and drizzle with oil. Continue cooking for another 20–30 minutes, or until the chicken is cooked through.

4 Sprinkle the remaining herbs over the chicken, then carve into portions. Thicken the sauce with a little cornstarch if you like.

Chicken Stroganoff

Based on the classic Russian dish, usually made with beef. Serve with rice mixed with chopped celery and scallions.

Serves 4

4 large chicken breasts, boned and skinned
3 tablespoons olive oil
1 large onion, thinly sliced
3 cups mushrooms, sliced
1¼ cups sour cream
salt and black pepper
1 tablespoon chopped fresh parsley, to garnish

1 Split the chicken breasts into two natural fillets, place between two sheets of plastic wrap and flatten each to a thickness of ½ inch with a rolling pin.

2 Cut into 1-inch strips diagonally across the fillets.

3 Heat 2 tablespoons of the oil in a frying pan and cook the onion slowly until soft but not colored.

4 Add the mushrooms and cook until golden brown. Remove and keep warm.

5 Increase the heat, add the remaining oil and fry the chicken very quickly, in small batches, for 3–4 minutes, until lightly colored. Remove to a dish and keep warm.

6 Return all the chicken, onions and mushrooms to the pan and season with salt and black pepper. Stir in the sour cream and bring to a boil. Sprinkle with fresh parsley and serve immediately.

Chicken Pancakes

A good way of using up leftover cooked chicken and frozen pancakes.

Serves 4

8 ounces cooked, boned chicken

2 tablespoons butter

1 small onion, finely chopped

$^3/_4$ cup mushrooms, finely chopped

2 tablespoons all-purpose flour

$^2/_3$ cup homemade or canned chicken stock or milk

1 tablespoon chopped fresh parsley

8 small or 4 large cooked pancakes

oil, for brushing

2 tablespoons grated cheese

salt and black pepper

1 Remove the skin from the chicken and cut into cubes.

2 Heat the butter in a saucepan and cook the onion gently until tender. Add the mushrooms. Cook, covered, for another 3–4 minutes.

3 Add the flour and then the stock or milk, stirring constantly. Boil to thicken and simmer for 2 minutes. Season with salt and black pepper.

4 Add the chicken cubes and chopped fresh parsley.

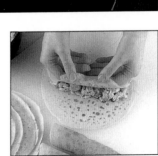

5 Divide the filling equally between the pancakes, roll up and arrange in a greased oven-proof dish. Preheat the broiler.

6 Brush the pancakes with a little oil and sprinkle with cheese. Broil until browned. Serve hot.

Lemon Chicken Stir-fry

It is essential to prepare all the ingredients before you begin so they are ready to cook. This dish is cooked in minutes.

INGREDIENTS

Serves 4

4 chicken breasts, boned and skinned
1 tablespoon light soy sauce
5 tablespoons cornstarch
1 bunch scallions
1 lemon
1 garlic clove, crushed
1 tablespoon sugar
2 tablespoons sherry
2/3 cup homemade or canned
   chicken stock
4 tablespoons olive oil
salt and black pepper

1 Split the chicken breasts into two natural fillets. Place each between two sheets of plastic wrap and flatten to a thickness of 1/4 inch with a rolling pin.

2 Cut into 1-inch strips across the grain of the fillets. Put in a bowl with the soy sauce and toss to coat. Sprinkle on 4 tablespoons of the cornstarch and toss.

3 Trim off the roots and cut the scallions diagonally into 1/2-inch pieces. With a vegetable peeler, remove the lemon rind in thin strips and cut into fine shreds, or grate finely. Reserve the lemon juice. Blend the garlic, sugar, sherry, stock, lemon juice and remaining cornstarch into a paste, with water.

4 Heat the oil in a wok or large frying pan and cook the chicken very quickly in small batches for 3–4 minutes, until lightly colored. Remove to a dish and keep warm.

5 Add the scallions and garlic to the pan and cook for 2 minutes.

6 Add the remaining ingredients, with the chicken, and bring to a boil, stirring until thickened. Add more sherry or stock, if necessary, and stir until the chicken is evenly covered with sauce. Reheat for about 2 minutes.

Crispy Spring Chickens

These small birds can be roasted in the oven fairly quickly and are delicious either hot or cold.

INGREDIENTS

Serves 4
2 chickens, 2 pounds each
salt and black pepper

For the honey glaze
2 tablespoons honey
2 tablespoons sherry
1 tablespoon vinegar

1 Preheat the oven to 350°F. Tie the birds into a neat shape and place on a wire rack over the sink. Pour boiling water over them to plump the flesh and pat dry with paper towels.

2 Mix the honey, sherry and vinegar together and brush over the birds. Season well.

3 Put the rack into a roasting pan and roast the birds for 45–55 minutes. Baste well during cooking with the honey glaze until crisp and golden brown.

Chicken Cordon Bleu

A rich dish, popular with cheese lovers. Serve simply with green beans and tiny baked potatoes, cut and filled with cream cheese.

INGREDIENTS

Serves 4

4 chicken breasts, boned and
   skinned
4 slices lean ham
4 tablespoons grated Gruyère or
   Emmental cheese
2 tablespoons olive oil
1^{1}/$_{4}$ cups button mushrooms, sliced
4 tablespoons white wine
salt and black pepper
watercress, to garnish

1 Place the chicken between two pieces of plastic wrap and flatten to a thickness of ^{1}/$_{4}$ inch with a rolling pin. Place the chicken breasts, outer side down, on the board and lay a slice of ham on each. Divide the cheese between the chicken breasts and season with a little salt and freshly ground pepper.

2 Fold the chicken breasts in half and secure with wooden toothpicks, making a large "stitch" to hold the pieces together.

3 Heat the oil in a large frying pan and brown the chicken breasts on all sides. Remove to a dish and keep warm.

4 Add the mushrooms to the pan and cook for several minutes to brown lightly. Replace the chicken and pour in the wine, cover, and cook gently for 15–20 minutes, until tender. Remove the toothpicks and arrange on a serving dish with a bunch of watercress.

Chicken in Herb Crusts

*The chicken breasts can be brushed
with melted butter instead of
mustard before being coated in the
breadcrumb mixture. Serve with
new potatoes and salad.*

Serves 4

4 chicken breasts, boned and skinned

1 tablespoon Dijon mustard

1 cup fresh breadcrumbs

2 tablespoons chopped fresh parsley

1 tablespoon mixed dried herbs

2 tablespoons butter, melted

salt and black pepper

2 Mix the breadcrumbs and
herbs together thoroughly.

3 Press onto the chicken to coat.
Spoon on the melted butter.
Bake uncovered for 20 minutes, or
until tender and crisp.

1 Preheat the oven to 350°F. Lay
the chicken breasts in a greased
ovenproof dish and spread with
the mustard. Season with salt and
freshly ground black pepper.

Tandoori Chicken Kebabs

This dish originated on the plains of the Punjab at the foot of the Himalayas. There, food is tradition-ally cooked in clay ovens known as tandoors – hence the name.

INGREDIENTS

Serves 4

4 chicken breasts, about 6 ounces each, boned and skinned

1 tablespoon lemon juice

3 tablespoons tandoori paste, available at Indian stores and some supermarkets

3 tablespoons plain yogurt

1 garlic clove, crushed

2 tablespoons chopped cilantro

1 small onion, cut into wedges and separated into layers

a little oil, for brushing

salt and black pepper

cilantro sprigs, to garnish

pilaf rice and naan bread, to serve

1 Chop the chicken breasts into 1-inch cubes, place in a bowl and add the lemon juice, tandoori paste, yogurt, garlic, cilantro and seasoning. Cover and let marinate in the fridge for at least 2–3 hours.

2 Preheat the broiler. Thread alternate pieces of chicken and onion onto four skewers.

3 Brush the onions with a little oil, lay the kebabs on a broiler rack and cook under high heat for about 10–12 minutes, turning once. Garnish the kebabs with cilantro and serve at once with pilaf rice and naan bread.

Chinese Chicken with Cashew Nuts

A stir-fry of chicken with egg noodles, scallions and cashews.

INGREDIENTS

Serves 4

4 chicken breasts about 6 ounces each, boned, skinned and sliced into strips

3 garlic cloves, crushed

4 tablespoons soy sauce

2 tablespoons cornstarch

1 cup dried egg noodles

3 tablespoons peanut or sunflower oil

1 tablespoon sesame oil

1 cup roasted cashews

6 scallions, cut into 2-inch pieces and halved lengthwise

scallion curls and a little chopped red chili, to garnish

4 Add the cashews and scallions to the pan and stir-fry for 2–3 minutes.

1 Put the chicken, garlic, soy sauce and cornstarch in a bowl and mix well. Cover and chill for about 30 minutes.

2 Bring a pan of water to a boil and add the noodles. Turn off the heat and let stand for 5 minutes. Drain well and reserve.

3 Heat the oils in a large frying pan and add the chicken and marinade. Stir-fry for about 3–4 minutes, or until golden brown.

5 Add the drained noodles and stir-fry for another 2 minutes. Serve immediately, garnished with the scallion curls and chopped red chili.

Broiled Rock Cornish Hens with Herbs

Allow one bird per person. Serve with boiled new potatoes and salad.

INGREDIENTS

Serves 4

4 Rock Cornish hens

4 tablespoons butter, melted

1 tablespoon lemon juice

1 tablespoon chopped mixed fresh herbs,
    such as rosemary and parsley,
    plus extra to garnish

salt and black pepper

lemon slices, to garnish

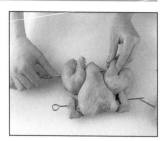

1 Remove any trussing strings and, using a pair of kitchen scissors, cut down on either side of the backbone and remove it. Lay the birds flat and flatten with the help of a rolling pin or mallet.

2 Thread the legs and wings onto skewers to keep the hens flat while they are cooking.

3 Brush both sides with melted butter and season with salt and pepper to taste. Sprinkle with lemon juice and herbs.

4 Preheat the broiler to medium heat and cook skin-side first for 6 minutes, until golden brown. Turn over, brush with butter and broil for another 6–8 minutes, or until cooked. Garnish with more chopped herbs and lemon slices.

Chicken Véronique

*True broiling chickens weigh about
2 pounds. If you can't find them, get
the smallest fryers you can.*

INGREDIENTS

Serves 4

2 broiling chickens, about 2 pounds each

2 fresh tarragon or thyme sprigs

2 tablespoons butter

4 tablespoons white wine

grated rind and juice of $^1/_2$ lemon

1 tablespoon olive oil

1 tablespoon all-purpose flour

$^2/_3$ cup homemade/canned chicken stock

1 cup seedless green grapes,
   cut in half if large

salt and black pepper

chopped fresh parsley, to garnish

1 Preheat the oven to 350°F.
Put the herbs inside the cavity
of each chicken and tie into a
neat shape.

2 Heat the butter in a casserole,
brown the chickens lightly all
over and pour on the wine. Season,
cover, and cook in the oven for
20–30 minutes, or until tender.

3 Remove the chickens from the
casserole and cut in half with a
pair of kitchen scissors, removing
the backbones and small rib cage
bones. Arrange in a shallow ovenproof dish (that will slide under
the broiler). Sprinkle with lemon
juice and brush with oil. Broil until
lightly browned. Keep warm.

4 Mix the flour into the butter
and wine in the casserole,
and blend in the stock. Bring to a
boil, season to taste, add the lemon
rind and grapes, then simmer for
2–3 minutes. Spoon the sauce on
the chickens, garnish with fresh
parsley and serve immediately.

Chicken with Orange and Mustard Sauce

The beauty of this recipe is its simplicity; the chicken continues to cook in its own juices while you prepare the sauce.

INGREDIENTS

Serves 4

4 chicken breasts, boned and skinned

1 teaspoon sunflower oil

salt and black pepper

new potatoes and sliced zucchini
tossed in parsley, to serve

Orange and mustard sauce

2 large oranges

2 teaspoons cornstarch

$2/3$ cup plain yogurt

1 teaspoon Dijon mustard

1 Peel the oranges, using a sharp knife, removing all the white pith. Remove the segments by cutting between the membranes, holding the fruit over a small bowl to catch any juice. Set aside with the juice until needed.

2 Season the chicken with salt and freshly ground black pepper. Heat the oil in a nonstick frying pan and cook the chicken breasts for 5 minutes on each side. Take out of the frying pan and wrap in foil; the meat will continue to cook for awhile.

3 To make the sauce, blend together the cornstarch with the juice from the oranges. Add the yogurt and mustard. Put into the frying pan and slowly bring to a boil. Simmer for 1 minute.

4 Add the orange segments to the sauce and heat gently. Unwrap the chicken and add any excess juices to the sauce. Slice on the diagonal and serve with the sauce, new potatoes and sliced zucchini tossed in parsley.

Chicken and Chorizo

The perfect way to use up leftover cold meat – this spicy dish is a fast, fortifying meal for a hungry family.

INGREDIENTS

Serves 4

3 tablespoons vegetable oil

1 medium onion, chopped

1 celery stalk, chopped

$^1/_2$ red bell pepper, chopped

2 cups long-grain rice

4 cups homemade/canned chicken stock

1 tablespoon tomato paste

3–4 shakes of Tabasco sauce

8 ounces cold roast chicken or pork, thickly sliced

4 ounces cooked sausage, such as chorizo or Polish, sliced

3 ounces frozen peas

3 Stir in the cold meat, sausage and peas and simmer for another 5 minutes. Switch off the heat, cover and let stand for 5 minutes more before serving.

VARIATIONS

You could also add cooked ham, smoked cod or haddock and fresh shellfish to this dish.

1 Heat the oil in a heavy-bottomed saucepan and add the onion, celery and pepper. Cook to soften, without coloring.

2 Add the rice, chicken stock, tomato paste and Tabasco sauce. Simmer uncovered for about 10 minutes.

Chicken Cutlets with Olives

This quick and tasty dish makes a good light main course.

INGREDIENTS

Serves 4

6 tablespoons olive oil

1 clove garlic, peeled and lightly
   crushed

1 dried chili, lightly crushed

1 1/4 pounds boneless chicken breast,
   cut into 1/4-inch slices

1/2 cup dry white wine

4 tomatoes, peeled and seeded,
   cut into thin strips

about 24 black olives

6–8 leaves fresh basil, torn into pieces

salt and black pepper

1 Heat 4 tablespoons of the olive oil in a large frying pan. Add the garlic and crushed dried chili, and cook over low heat until the garlic is golden.

2 Raise the heat to medium and add remaining oil. Place the chicken slices in the pan, and brown them lightly on both sides for about 2 minutes. Season with salt and pepper. Remove the chicken to a heated dish.

3 Discard the garlic and chili. Add the wine, tomato strips and olives. Cook over medium heat for 3–4 minutes, scraping up any residue from the bottom of the pan.

4 Return the chicken to the pan. Sprinkle with the torn basil. Heat through for 30 seconds, and serve at once.

Mediterranean Chicken Skewers

These skewers are easy to assemble, and can be cooked under the broiler or on a charcoal grill.

INGREDIENTS

Serves 4

6 tablespoons olive oil

3 tablespoons fresh lemon juice

1 clove garlic, finely chopped

2 tablespoons chopped fresh basil

2 medium zucchini

1 long thin eggplant

11 ounces boneless chicken, cut into
    2-inch cubes

12–16 pickled onions

1 bell pepper, red or yellow, cut into
    2-inch squares

salt and black pepper

1 In a small bowl, mix the oil with the lemon juice, garlic and basil. Season with salt and pepper.

2 Slice the zucchini and eggplant lengthwise into strips ¼-inch thick. Cut them horizontally about two-thirds of the way along their length. Discard the shorter length. Wrap half the chicken pieces with the zucchini slices, and the other half with the eggplant slices.

3 Prepare the skewers by alternating the chicken, onions and pepper pieces. Lay the prepared skewers on a platter, and sprinkle with the flavored oil. Let marinate for at least 30 minutes. Preheat the broiler, or prepare a charcoal grill.

4 Broil or grill for about 10 minutes, or until the vegetables are tender, turning the skewers occasionally. Serve hot.

Rock Cornish Hens with Dirty Rice

This rice is called dirty not because of the bits in it (though the roux and chicken livers do "muss" it up a bit) but because jazz is called "dirty music," and the rice in this recipe is certainly jazzed up.

INGREDIENTS

Serves 4

For the rice

4 tablespoons cooking oil

$^{1}/_{4}$ cup all-purpose flour

4 tablespoons butter

1 large onion, chopped

2 celery stalks, chopped

1 green bell pepper, seeded and diced

2 garlic cloves, crushed

7 ounces ground pork

8 ounces chicken livers, trimmed
    and sliced

Tabasco sauce

$1^{1}/_{4}$ cups homemade or canned
    chicken stock

4 scallions, shredded

3 tablespoons chopped fresh parsley

1 cup American long-grain
    rice, cooked

salt and black pepper

For the birds

4 Rock Cornish hens

2 bay leaves, halved

2 tablespoons butter

1 lemon

COOK'S TIP

If available, try substituting quails for the Rock Cornish hens, in which case offer two per person and stuff each little bird with 2 teaspoons of dirty rice before roasting for about 20 minutes.

---

1 In a small heavy-bottomed saucepan, make a roux by blending together 2 tablespoons of the oil and the flour. When it is a chestnut brown color, remove the pan from the heat and place it immediately on a cold surface.

2 Heat the remaining 2 tablespoons oil with the butter in a frying pan and stir-fry the onion, celery and green bell pepper for about 5 minutes.

3 Add the garlic and pork and stir-fry for about 5 minutes, breaking up the pork and stirring well to cook it all over.

4 Add the chicken livers and fry for 2–3 minutes until they have changed color all over. Season with salt and black pepper and a dash of Tabasco sauce.

5 Stir the roux into the stir-fried mixture, then gradually add the stock. When it begins to bubble, cover and cook for 30 minutes, stirring occasionally. Uncover and cook for another 15 minutes, stirring frequently.

6 Preheat the oven to 400°F. Mix the shredded scallions and chopped parsley into the meat mixture and stir it all into the cooked rice.

7 Put $^{1}/_{2}$ bay leaf and 1 tablespoon rice into each bird. Rub the outside with the butter and season with salt and pepper.

8 Put the birds on a rack in a roasting pan, squeeze the juice from the lemon over them and roast in the oven for 35–40 minutes, basting twice during cooking with the pan juices.

9 Put the remaining rice into a shallow ovenproof dish, cover it and place on a low rack in the oven for the last 15–20 minutes of the birds' cooking time.

10 Serve the birds on a bed of dirty rice with the roasting juices (drained of fat) poured on top.

Chicken Kiev

Cut through the crispy-coated chicken to reveal a creamy filling with just a hint of garlic.

INGREDIENTS

Serves 4

4 large chicken breasts, boned and
    skinned
1 tablespoon lemon juice
$1/2$ cup ricotta cheese
1 garlic clove, crushed
2 tablespoons chopped fresh parsley
$1/4$ teaspoon freshly grated nutmeg
2 tablespoons all-purpose flour
pinch of cayenne pepper
$1/4$ teaspoon salt
2 cups fresh white breadcrumbs
2 egg whites, lightly beaten
creamed potatoes, green beans and
    broiled tomatoes, to serve

1 Preheat the oven to 400°F. Place the chicken breasts between two sheets of plastic wrap and gently beat with a rolling pin until flattened. Sprinkle with the lemon juice.

2 Mix the ricotta cheese with the garlic, 1 tablespoon of the chopped parsley and the nutmeg. Shape into four 2-inch long rolls.

3 Put one portion of the cheese and herb mixture in the center of each chicken breast and fold the meat over, tucking in the edges to enclose the filling completely.

4 Secure the chicken with tooth-picks pushed through the center of each. Mix together the flour, cayenne pepper and salt and use to dust the chicken.

5 Mix together the breadcrumbs and remaining parsley. Dip the chicken into the egg whites, then coat with the breadcrumbs. Chill for 30 minutes in the fridge, then dip into the egg white and bread-crumbs for a second time.

6 Put the chicken on a nonstick baking sheet. Bake in the pre-heated oven for 25 minutes, or until the coating is golden brown and the chicken completely cooked. Remove the toothpicks and serve with creamed potatoes, green beans and broiled tomatoes.

Stuffed Rock Cornish Hens

Port wine-soaked raisins, walnuts and mushrooms make an unusual stuffing for Rock Cornish hens.

INGREDIENTS

Serves 4

1 cup Port wine

$^1/_3$ cup raisins

1 tablespoon walnut oil

3 ounces mushrooms, minced

1 large celery stalk, minced

1 small onion, chopped

salt and pepper

1 cup fresh breadcrumbs

$^1/_2$ cup chopped walnuts

1 tablespoon each chopped fresh
    basil and parsley, or 2 tablespoons
    chopped parsley

$^1/_2$ teaspoon dried thyme

6 tablespoons butter, melted

4 Rock Cornish hens

1 Preheat the oven to 350°F.

2 In a small bowl, combine the Port wine and raisins and let soak for about 20 minutes.

3 Meanwhile, heat the oil in a nonstick pan. Add the mushrooms, celery, onion and $^1/_4$ teaspoon salt and cook over low heat until softened, about 8–10 minutes. Set aside to cool.

4 Drain the raisins, reserving the Port wine. Combine the raisins, breadcrumbs, walnuts, basil, parsley and thyme in a bowl. Stir in the onion mixture and 4 tablespoons of the melted butter. Add $^1/_2$ teaspoon salt and pepper to taste.

5 Fill the cavity of each bird with the stuffing. Do not pack down. Tie the legs together, to enclose the stuffing securely.

6 Brush the birds with the remaining butter and place in a baking dish just large enough to hold them comfortably. Pour on the reserved Port wine.

7 Roast, basting occasionally, for about 1 hour. Test by piercing the thigh with a skewer; the juices should run clear. Serve immediately with some of the juices.

Oven "Fried" Chicken

The chicken in this dish is not fried but baked until crisp in the oven.

Serves 4

4 large chicken pieces
1/2 cup flour
1/2 teaspoon salt
1/4 teaspoon pepper
1 egg
2 tablespoons water
2 tablespoons chopped mixed fresh herbs,
  such as parsley, basil and thyme
1 cup dry breadcrumbs
1/3 cup freshly grated
  Parmesan cheese
lemon wedges, for serving

1 Preheat the oven to 400°F.

2 Rinse the chicken in cold water. Pat dry with paper towels.

3 Combine the flour, salt and pepper on a plate and stir with a fork to mix. Coat the chicken pieces on all sides with the flour and shake off the excess.

4 Sprinkle a little water onto the chicken pieces, and coat again lightly with the seasoned flour.

5 Beat the egg with the water in a shallow dish. Stir in the herbs. Dip the chicken pieces into the egg mixture, turning them over to coat them thoroughly.

6 Combine the breadcrumbs and grated Parmesan cheese on a plate. Roll the chicken pieces in the crumbs, patting with your fingers to help them adhere.

7 Place the chicken pieces in a greased shallow pan, large enough to hold them in one layer. Bake until thoroughly cooked and golden brown, 20–30 minutes. To check that they are cooked, prick with a fork; the juices that run out should be clear, not pink. Serve hot, with lemon wedges.

Blackened Chicken Breasts

Chicken breasts with a seasoned coating of herbs and spices.

INGREDIENTS

Serves 6

6 medium chicken breasts,
 boned and skinned
6 tablespoons butter or margarine
1 teaspoon garlic paste
4 tablespoons finely grated onion
1 teaspoon cayenne
2 teaspoons sweet paprika
1¹/₂ teaspoons salt
¹/₂ teaspoon white pepper
1 teaspoon black pepper
¹/₄ teaspoon ground cumin
1 teaspoon dried thyme leaves

1 Slice each chicken breast piece in half horizontally. Flatten them down slightly with the heel of your hand.

2 Melt the butter or margarine in a small saucepan together with the garlic paste.

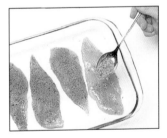

3 Combine all the remaining ingredients in a shallow bowl and stir well. Brush the chicken pieces on both sides with melted butter or margarine, then sprinkle evenly with the seasoned mixture.

4 Heat a large heavy frying pan over high heat until a drop of water sprinkled on the surface sizzles. This will take 5–8 minutes.

5 Drizzle 1 teaspoon of melted butter on each chicken piece. Place them in the pan in an even layer, 2 or 3 at a time. Cook until the underside begins to blacken, about 2–3 minutes. Turn over and cook 2–3 minutes more, or until the other side blackens. Serve hot.

Chicken Tonnato

This low-fat version of the Italian dish "vitello tonnato" is garnished with fine strips of red pepper instead of the traditional anchovy fillets.

INGREDIENTS

Serves 4

1 pound chicken breasts, boned
   and skinned
1 small onion, sliced
1 bay leaf
4 black peppercorns
1¹/₂ cup homemade/canned chicken stock
7-ounce can tuna in water, drained
5 tablespoons reduced fat mayonnaise
2 tablespoons lemon juice
2 red bell peppers, thinly sliced
about 25 capers, drained
pinch of salt
mixed salad and tomatoes, to serve

4 Put the tuna, mayonnaise, lemon juice, 3 tablespoons of the reduced stock and salt into a blender or food processor and purée until smooth.

5 Stir in enough of the remaining stock to reduce the sauce to the thickness of heavy cream. Spoon onto the chicken.

6 Arrange the strips of red pepper in a lattice pattern over the chicken. Put a caper in the center of each square. Chill in the fridge for 1 hour and serve with a fresh mixed salad and tomatoes.

1 Put the chicken breasts in a single layer in a large, heavy-bottomed saucepan. Add the onion, bay leaf, peppercorns and stock. Bring to a boil and reduce the heat. Cover and simmer for about 12 minutes, or until tender.

2 Turn off the heat and let the chicken cool in the stock, then remove with a slotted spoon. Slice the breasts thickly and arrange on a serving plate.

3 Boil the stock until it is reduced to about 5 table-spoons. Strain through a fine sieve and cool.

Chicken and Tomato Hot-pot

*Versatile ground chicken is perfect
for family meals. Here, it's turned
into tasty meatballs.*

INGREDIENTS

Serves 4

1 slice white bread, crust removed

2 tablespoons milk

1 garlic clove, crushed

$^1/_2$ teaspoon caraway seeds

2 cups ground chicken

1 egg white

1$^1/_2$ cups homemade or canned
   chicken stock

14-ounce can plum tomatoes

1 tablespoon tomato paste

$^1/_2$ cup long-grain rice

salt and black pepper

1 tablespoon chopped fresh basil

carrot and zucchini ribbons, to serve

4 Put the chicken stock, tomatoes and tomato paste into a
large, heavy-bottomed saucepan
and bring to a boil.

5 Add the rice, stir, and cook
briskly for about 5 minutes.
Turn the heat down to a simmer.

6 Meanwhile, shape the chicken
mixture into 16 small balls.
Carefully drop them into the
tomato stock and simmer for
another 8–10 minutes, or until the
chicken balls and rice are cooked.
Garnish with the basil, and serve
with carrot and zucchini ribbons.

1 Cut the bread into small cubes
and put into a mixing bowl.
Sprinkle with the milk and let soak
for 5 minutes.

2 Add the garlic clove, caraway
seeds, chicken, salt and freshly
ground black pepper to the bread.
Mix together well.

3 Beat the egg white until stiff,
then fold, in two parts, into the
chicken mixture. Chill for
10 minutes in the fridge.

Roast Chicken with Fennel

In Italy this dish is prepared with wild fennel. Cultivated fennel bulb works just as well.

INGREDIENTS

Serves 4–5

1 roasting chicken, about 3$\frac{1}{2}$ pounds
1 onion, quartered
$\frac{1}{2}$ cup olive oil
2 medium fennel bulbs
1 clove garlic, peeled
pinch of grated nutmeg
3–4 thin slices pancetta or bacon
$\frac{1}{2}$ cup dry white wine
salt and black pepper

1 Preheat the oven to 350°F. Sprinkle the chicken cavity with salt and pepper. Place the onion quarters in the cavity. Rub the chicken with about 3 tablespoons of the olive oil. Place in a roasting pan.

2 Cut the green fronds from the tops of the fennel bulbs. Chop the fronds together with the garlic. Place in a small bowl and mix with the nutmeg and seasoning.

3 Sprinkle the fennel mixture over the chicken, pressing it on the oiled skin. Cover the breast with the slices of pancetta or bacon. Sprinkle with 2 tablespoons of the oil. Place in the oven and roast for 30 minutes.

4 Meanwhile, boil or steam the fennel bulbs until barely tender. Remove from the heat and cut into quarters or sixths length-wise. After the chicken has been cooking for 30 minutes, remove the pan from the oven. Baste the chicken with any oils in the pan.

5 Arrange the fennel pieces around the chicken. Sprinkle the fennel with the remaining oil. Pour about half the wine on the chicken, and return to the oven.

6 After 30 minutes more, baste the chicken again. Pour on the remaining wine. Cook for 15–20 minutes. To test, prick the thigh with a fork. If the juices run clear, the chicken is cooked. Serve the chicken surrounded by the fennel.

Chicken with Ham and Cheese

This tasty combination comes from Emilia-Romagna, where it is also prepared with veal.

INGREDIENTS

Serves 4

4 small chicken breasts, skinned
    and boned
flour seasoned with salt and freshly
    ground black pepper, for dredging
4 tablespoons butter
3–4 leaves fresh sage
4 thin slices prosciutto or ham, cut in half
$\frac{1}{2}$ cup freshly grated
    Parmesan cheese

1 Cut each breast in half length-wise to make two flat fillets of approximately the same thickness. Dredge the chicken in the seasoned flour, and shake off the excess.

2 Preheat the broiler. Heat the butter in a large heavy frying pan and add the sage leaves. Add the chicken, in one layer, and cook over low to medium heat until golden brown on both sides, turning as necessary. This will take about 15 minutes.

3 Remove the chicken from the heat, and arrange on a flame-proof serving dish or broiler pan. Place one piece of ham on each chicken fillet and top with the grated Parmesan. Broil for 3–4 minutes, or until the cheese has melted. Serve at once.

Chicken Roll

The roll can be prepared and cooked the day before and will freeze well too. Remove from the fridge about an hour before serving.

INGREDIENTS

Serves 8

1 chicken, about 4$^{1}/_{2}$ pounds

For the stuffing

1 medium onion, finely chopped

4 tablespoons melted butter

2 cups lean ground pork

4 ounces lean bacon, chopped

1 tablespoon chopped fresh parsley

2 teaspoons chopped fresh thyme

2 cups fresh white breadcrumbs

2 tablespoons sherry

1 large egg, beaten

$^{1}/_{4}$ cup shelled pistachios

$^{1}/_{4}$ cup pitted black olives
    (about 12)

salt and black pepper

1 To make the stuffing, cook the chopped onion gently in 2 tablespoons of the butter until soft. Put into a bowl and cool. Add the remaining ingredients, mix thoroughly and season with salt and black pepper.

2 To bone the chicken, use a small, sharp knife to remove the wing tips. Turn the chicken onto its breast and cut a line down the backbone.

3 Cut the meat away from the carcass, scraping the bones clean. Carefully cut through the sinew around the leg and wing joints and scrape down the bones to free them. Remove the carcass, taking care not to cut through the skin along the breastbone.

4 To stuff the chicken, lay it flat, skin side down and flatten as much as possible. Shape the stuffing down the center of the chicken and fold in the sides.

5 Sew the bird neatly together, using a needle and dark thread. Tie with fine string into a roll.

6 Preheat the oven to 350°F. Put the roll, seam side down, on a rack in a roasting pan and brush with the remaining butter. Cook, uncovered, for about 1$^{1}/_{4}$ hours. Baste with the juices during cooking. Let cool. Remove the string and thread. Wrap in foil and chill until needed.

Traditional Roast Chicken

Serve with bacon rolls, small sausages, gravy and stuffing balls.

INGREDIENTS

Serves 4

1 chicken, about 4 pounds
lean bacon strips
2 tablespoons butter
salt and black pepper

For the prune and nut stuffing
2 tablespoons butter
$^1/_2$ cup chopped pitted prunes
$^1/_2$ cup chopped walnuts
1 cup fresh breadcrumbs
1 egg, beaten
1 tablespoon chopped fresh parsley
1 tablespoon chopped fresh chives
2 tablespoons sherry or Port

For the gravy
2 tablespoons all-purpose flour
$1^1/_4$ cups homemade or canned
    chicken stock

1 Preheat the oven to 375°F. Mix all the stuffing ingredients in a bowl and season well with salt and pepper.

2 Stuff the neck end of the chicken quite loosely, allowing room for the breadcrumbs to swell during cooking. (Any remaining stuffing can be shaped into balls and fried to accompany the roast.)

3 Tuck the neck skin under the bird to secure the stuffing and hold in place with the wing tips, or sew with strong thread or fine string.

4 Place in a roasting pan and cover the breast with the bacon strips. Spread with the remaining butter, cover loosely with foil and roast for about 1$^1/_2$ hours. Baste with the juices in the roasting pan 3 or 4 times during cooking.

5 Remove any trussing string, transfer to a serving plate, cover with foil and let stand while making the gravy. (This standing time allows the flesh to relax and makes carving easier.)

6 Spoon off the fat from the juices in the pan. Blend in the flour and cook gently until golden brown. Add the stock and bring to a boil, stirring until thickened. Adjust the seasoning and strain into a sauceboat to serve.

Roast Chicken with Celery Root

Chicken with a stuffing of celery root, bacon, onion and herbs.

INGREDIENTS

Serves 4

1 chicken, 3^1/$_2$ pounds
1 tablespoon butter

For the stuffing

1 pound celery root, chopped
2 tablespoons butter
3 slices bacon, chopped
1 onion, finely chopped
leaves from 1 thyme sprig, chopped
leaves from 1 small tarragon
 sprig, chopped
2 tablespoons chopped
 fresh parsley
1^1/$_2$ cups fresh brown breadcrumbs
dash of Worcestershire sauce
1 egg, beaten
salt and pepper

1 For the stuffing, cook the celery root in boiling water until tender. Drain well and chop finely.

2 Heat the butter in a saucepan, then gently cook the bacon and onion until the onion is soft. Stir the celery root and herbs into the pan and cook, stirring occasionally, for 2–3 minutes. Meanwhile, preheat the oven to 400°F.

3 Remove the pan from the heat and stir in the fresh bread-crumbs, Worcestershire sauce, seasoning and sufficient egg to bind.

4 Place the stuffing in the neck end of the chicken. Season the bird's skin, then rub with the butter. Roast the chicken, basting occasionally with the juices, for 1^1/$_4$–1^1/$_2$ hours, until the juices run clear when the thickest part of the leg is pierced. Rest for 10 minutes in a warm place before carving.

Rock Cornish Hens with Grapes in Vermouth

A very special dish, ideal to serve when entertaining.

Serves 4

4 oven-ready Rock Cornish hens, about
    1 pound each
4 tablespoons butter, softened
2 shallots, chopped
4 tablespoons chopped fresh parsley
8 ounces white grapes, preferably
    muscatel, halved and seeded
$2/3$ cup white vermouth
1 teaspoon cornstarch
4 tablespoons heavy cream
2 tablespoons pine nuts, toasted
salt and black pepper
watercress sprigs, to garnish

1 Preheat the oven to 400°F. Spread the softened butter all over the hens and put a hazelnut-sized piece inside the cavity of each bird.

2 Mix together the shallots and parsley and place a quarter of the mixture inside each hen. Put the birds side by side in a large roasting pan and roast for 40–50 minutes, or until the juices run clear when the thickest part of the flesh is pierced with a skewer. Put the birds onto a warm serving dish, cover and keep warm.

3 Skim off most of the fat from the roasting pan, then add the grapes and vermouth. Place the pan directly over a low flame for a few minutes to warm and slightly soften the grapes.

4 Lift the grapes out of the pan using a slotted spoon and sprinkle them around the birds. Keep covered. Stir the cornstarch into the cream, then add to the pan juices. Cook gently for a few minutes, stirring, until the sauce has thickened. Adjust seasoning.

5 Pour the sauce around the birds. Sprinkle with the toasted pine nuts and garnish with watercress sprigs.

Stir-fried Chicken with Snow Peas

Juicy chicken stir-fried with snow peas, cashews and water chestnuts.

INGREDIENTS

Serves 4

2 tablespoons sesame oil

6 tablespoons lemon juice

1 garlic clove, crushed

1/2-inch piece fresh ginger,
    peeled and grated

1 teaspoon honey

1 pound chicken breast fillets,
    cut into strips

4 ounces snow peas, trimmed

2 tablespoons peanut oil

1/2 cup cashews

6 scallions, cut into strips

1 can (8-ounces) water chestnuts,
    drained and thinly sliced

salt

saffron rice, to serve

1 Mix together the sesame oil, lemon juice, garlic, ginger and honey in a shallow non-metallic dish. Add the chicken and mix well. Cover and let marinate for at least 3–4 hours.

2 Blanch the snow peas in boiling salted water for 1 minute. Drain and refresh under cold running water.

3 Drain the chicken strips and reserve the marinade. Heat the peanut oil in a wok or large frying pan, add the cashews and stir-fry for about 1–2 minutes until golden brown. Remove the cashews from the wok or frying pan, using a slotted spoon, and set aside.

4 Add the chicken and stir-fry for 3–4 minutes, until golden brown. Add the scallions, snow peas, water chestnuts and the reserved marinade. Cook for a few minutes, until the chicken is tender and the sauce is bubbling and hot. Stir in the cashews and serve with saffron rice.

Stuffed Chicken Breasts with Cream Sauce

*Chicken breasts filled with a leek
and lime-flavored stuffing and
served in a cream sauce.*

INGREDIENTS

Serves 4

4 large chicken breasts,
  boned and skinned
4 tablespoons butter
3 large leeks, white and pale green
  parts only, thinly sliced
1 teaspoon grated lime zest
1 cup chicken stock, homemade or
  canned, or half stock and half
  dry white wine
$^1/_2$ cup whipping or
  heavy cream
1 tablespoon lime juice
salt and pepper

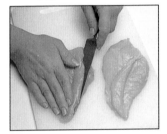

1 Cut horizontally into the
thickest part of each breast to
make a deep, wide pocket. Take
care not to cut all the way through.
Set the chicken breasts aside.

2 Melt half the butter in a large
heavy frying pan over low heat.
Add the leeks and lime zest and
cook, stirring occasionally, for
15–20 minutes, or until the leeks
are very soft but not colored.

3 Put the leeks in a bowl and
season to taste with salt and
pepper. Let cool. Wash and dry the
frying pan.

4 Divide the leeks among the
chicken breasts, packing the
pockets full. Secure the openings
with wooden toothpicks.

5 Melt the remaining butter in
the frying pan over medium
high heat. Add the stuffed breasts
and brown lightly on both sides.

6 Add the stock and bring to a
boil. Cover and simmer for
about 10 minutes, or until the
chicken is cooked through.
Carefully turn the breasts over
halfway through the cooking.

7 With a slotted spatula, remove
the breasts from the pan and
keep warm. Boil the cooking liquid
until it is reduced by half.

8 Stir the cream into the cooking
liquid and boil until reduced
by about half again. Stir in the lime
juice and season to taste.

9 Remove the toothpicks from
the breasts. Cut each breast on
the diagonal into $^1/_2$-inch slices,
pour the sauce over them and
serve.

VARIATION

For Onion-stuffed Chicken
Breasts, use 2 sweet onions, halved
and thinly sliced, instead of leeks.

Pasta with Chicken Livers

Chicken livers in a piquant sauce served with pasta.

INGREDIENTS

Serves 4

8 ounces chicken livers, defrosted
    if frozen
2 tablespoons olive oil
2 garlic cloves, crushed
6 ounces rindless Canadian bacon,
    coarsely chopped
14-ounce can chopped tomatoes
2/3 cup homemade or canned
    chicken stock
1 tablespoon tomato paste
1 tablespoon dry sherry
2 tablespoons chopped mixed fresh
    herbs, such as parsley, rosemary
    and basil
12 ounces dried orecchiette pasta
salt and black pepper
freshly grated Parmesan cheese, to serve

1 Wash and trim the chicken livers. Cut into bite-sized pieces. Heat the oil in a sauté pan and fry the chicken livers for 3–4 minutes, or until tender.

2 Add the garlic and bacon to the pan and fry until golden brown. Add the tomatoes, chicken stock, tomato paste, sherry, herbs and seasoning to taste.

3 Bring the sauce to the boil and simmer gently, uncovered, for about 5 minutes until the sauce has thickened. Stir from time to time.

4 Meanwhile, cook the pasta in boiling salted water for about 12 minutes until "al dente". Drain, then toss into the sauce. Serve hot, sprinkled with Parmesan cheese.

Chicken Baked in a Salt Crust

This unusual dish is extremely easy to make. Once it is cooked, you just break away the salt crust to reveal the wonderfully tender, golden brown chicken underneath.

INGREDIENTS

Serves 4

1 corn-fed or free-range oven-ready
    chicken, 3–3 1/2 pounds
bunch of mixed fresh herbs, such as
    rosemary, thyme, marjoram and parsley
7 cups coarse sea salt
1 egg white
1–2 whole heads of baked garlic,
    to serve

1 Preheat the oven to 350°F. Wipe the chicken. Put the herbs into the cavity, then truss the chicken.

2 Mix together the sea salt and egg white until all the salt crystals are moistened. Select a roasting pan into which the chicken will fit neatly, then line it with a large double layer of foil.

3 Spread a thick layer of the salt in the foil-lined pan and put the chicken on top. Cover with the remaining salt and shape neatly around the chicken, making sure it is completely enclosed.

4 Bring the foil edges up and over the chicken to enclose it and bake in the oven for 1 1/2 hours. Remove from the oven and let rest for 10 minutes.

5 Carefully lift the foil package from the pan and open. Break the salt crust and brush any traces of salt from the bird. Serve with baked whole heads of garlic. Slip each clove from its skin and eat with a bite of chicken.

Risotto with Chicken

This is a complete meal cooked conveniently all in one pan.

INGREDIENTS

Serves 4

2 tablespoons olive oil

8 ounces chicken breast, skinned, boned
   and cut into 1-inch cubes

1 onion, finely chopped

1 garlic clove, finely chopped

$1/4$ teaspoon saffron strands

$1/2$ cup Parma ham, cut
   into thin strips

2 cups risotto rice,
   preferably Arborio

$1/2$ cup dry white wine

$7^1/2$ cups simmering chicken stock,
   preferably homemade

2 tablespoons butter (optional)

$1/3$ cup freshly grated Parmesan cheese,
   plus more to serve

salt and pepper

1 Heat the oil in a wide heavy-bottomed pan over medium high heat. Add the chicken cubes and cook, stirring, until they start to turn white.

2 Reduce the heat to low. Add the onion, garlic, saffron and Parma ham. Cook, stirring, until the onion is soft. Stir in the risotto rice and mix well. Sauté for 1–2 minutes, stirring constantly.

3 Add the wine and bring to a boil. Simmer gently until almost all the wine is absorbed.

4 Add the simmering stock, a ladleful at a time, and cook, stirring constantly, until the rice is just tender and the risotto creamy.

5 Add the butter, if using, and Parmesan cheese and stir in well. Season with salt and pepper to taste. Serve the risotto hot, sprinkled with more Parmesan.

Cannelloni al Forno

*A lighter alternative to the usual
beef-filled, béchamel-coated version.
Fill with ricotta, onions and
mushrooms for a vegetarian recipe.*

INGREDIENTS

Serves 4–6

4 cups skinned and boned chicken
    breast, cooked
2 ¹/2 cups mushrooms
2 garlic cloves, crushed
2 tablespoons chopped fresh parsley
1 tablespoon chopped fresh tarragon
1 egg, beaten
fresh lemon juice
12–18 cannelloni tubes
2 cups homemade or canned
    tomato sauce
²/3 cup freshly grated Parmesan cheese
salt and pepper
1 sprig fresh parsley, to garnish

1 Preheat the oven to 400°F.
Place the chicken in a blender
or food processor and blend until
finely ground. Transfer to a bowl.

2 Place the mushrooms, garlic,
parsley and tarragon in the
food processor and blend until
finely ground.

3 Beat the mushroom mixture
into the chicken mixture thoroughly, then add the egg, salt and
pepper and lemon juice to taste
and mix well.

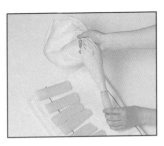

5 Place the filling in a pastry bag
fitted with a large plain nozzle.
Use this to fill each tube of
cannelloni, once they are cool
enough to handle.

6 Lay the filled cannelloni tightly
together in a single layer in a
buttered shallow ovenproof dish.
Spoon the tomato sauce over them
and sprinkle with Parmesan
cheese. Bake in the oven for
30 minutes, or until brown and
bubbling. Serve garnished with a
sprig of parsley.

Chicken and Curry Mayonnaise Sandwich

A very useful and appetizing way of using leftover pieces of chicken.

Serves 2

4 slices whole wheat bread
2 tablespoons softened butter
4 ounces cooked chicken, sliced
3 tablespoons Curry Mayonnaise
1 bunch watercress, trimmed

3 Arrange a few sprigs of watercress on top, cover with the remaining bread, press lightly together and cut in half.

CURRY MAYONNAISE

Makes about $^2/_3$ cup

$^1/_2$ cup mayonnaise
2 teaspoons concentrated bottled curry paste or good curry powder
$^1/_2$ teaspoon lemon juice
2 teaspoons sieved apricot jam

Combine all the ingredients thoroughly and chill until needed.

1 Spread the Curry Mayonnaise over the chicken slices.

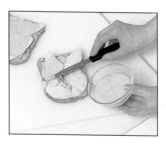

2 Spread the Curry Mayonnaise over the chicken slices.

Oriental Chicken Sandwich

*This filling is also good served in
warmed pita bread, in which case
cut the chicken into small cubes
before marinating. Broil on skewers
and serve warm.*

INGREDIENTS

Serves 2

1 tablespoon soy sauce
1 teaspoon honey
1 teaspoon sesame oil
1 garlic clove, crushed
6 ounces chicken breast,
   boned and skinned
4 slices white bread
4 tablespoons peanut butter
2 tablespoons beansprouts
1 ounce red bell pepper, seeded
   and finely sliced
2 sprigs parsley, to garnish

1 Mix together the soy sauce,
honey, sesame oil and garlic.
Brush on the chicken breast.

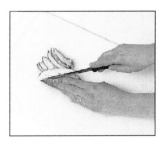

2 Broil the chicken for 3–4
minutes on each side until
cooked through, then slice thinly.

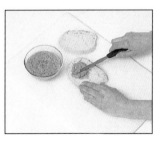

3 Spread two slices of the bread
with some of the peanut butter.

4 Arrange the slices of chicken
on top of the peanut butter.

5 Spread a little more peanut
butter over the chicken.

6 Sprinkle on the beansprouts
and red pepper and sandwich
together with the remaining slices
of bread. Cut in half, if desired.

Chicken and Shiitake Mushroom Pizza

The addition of shiitake mushrooms adds an earthy flavor to this colorful pizza, while fresh red chili gives a hint of spiciness.

INGREDIENTS

Serves 3–4

3 tablespoons olive oil

3 cups chicken breast fillets,
  skinned and cut into thin strips

1 bunch scallions, sliced

1 fresh red chili, seeded and chopped

1 red bell pepper, seeded and cut
  into thin strips

3 ounces fresh shiitake mushrooms,
  wiped and sliced

3–4 tablespoons chopped
  fresh cilantro

1 pizza crust, about 10–12 inches
  diameter

1 tablespoon chili oil

1¹/₄ cups mozzarella cheese

salt and black pepper

1 Preheat the oven to 425°F. Heat 2 tablespoons of the olive oil in a wok or large frying pan. Add the chicken, scallions, chili, pepper and mushrooms and stir-fry over high heat for 2–3 minutes, until the chicken is firm but still slightly pink in the center. Season with salt and pepper.

2 Pour off any excess oil, then set aside the chicken mixture until cool.

3 Stir the fresh cilantro into the chicken mixture.

4 Brush the pizza crust with the chili oil.

5 Spoon on the chicken mixture and drizzle on the remaining olive oil.

6 Grate the mozzarella and sprinkle on. Bake for 15–20 minutes, until crisp and golden. Serve immediately.

ONE POT
MEALS

Nasi Goreng

This dish is originally from Thailand and can be easily adapted by adding any cooked ingredients you have on hand. Crisp shrimp crackers make an ideal accompaniment.

Serves 4

1 cup long-grain rice
2 eggs
2 tablespoons vegetable oil
1 green chili
2 scallions, coarsely chopped
2 cloves garlic, crushed
8 ounces cooked chicken
8 ounces cooked shrimp
3 tablespoons dark soy sauce
shrimp crackers, to serve

1 Rinse the rice and then cook for 10–12 minutes in 2 cups water in a pan with a tight-fitting lid. When cooked, refresh under cold water.

2 Lightly beat the eggs. Heat 1 tablespoon of oil in a small frying pan and swirl in the beaten egg. When cooked on one side, flip the egg over and cook on the other. Remove from the pan and let cool. Cut the omelet into strips.

3 Carefully remove the seeds from the chili and chop finely, wearing rubber gloves to protect your hands, if necessary. Place the scallions, chili and garlic in a blender or food processor and blend to a paste.

4 Heat the wok, and then add the remaining oil. When the oil is hot, add the chili paste and stir-fry for 1 minute.

5 Stir the chicken and shrimp into the chili paste.

6 Add the rice and stir-fry for 3–4 minutes. Stir in the soy sauce and serve with shrimp crackers.

Chicken and Rice Vermicelli

This delicious dish makes a filling meal. Take care when frying vermicelli, as it has a tendency to spit when added to hot oil.

Serves 4

¹/₂ cup vegetable oil

8 ounces rice vermicelli

5 ounces green beans, ends removed and
    halved lengthwise

1 onion, finely chopped

2 chicken breasts, about 6 ounces each,
    boned, skinned and cut into strips

1 teaspoon cayenne pepper

8 ounces cooked shrimp

3 tablespoons dark soy sauce

3 tablespoons white wine vinegar

2 teaspoons sugar

cilantro sprigs, to garnish

1 Heat a wok or frying pan, then add 4 tablespoons of the oil. Break up the vermicelli into 3-inch lengths. When the oil is hot, fry the vermicelli in batches. Remove from the heat and keep warm.

2 Heat the remaining oil, then add the green beans, chopped onion and chicken and stir-fry for 3 minutes, until the chicken strips are cooked.

3 Sprinkle in the cayenne pepper. Stir in the cooked shrimp, soy sauce, vinegar and sugar, and stir-fry for 2 minutes.

4 Serve the chicken, shrimp and vegetables on the fried vermicelli, garnished with sprigs of cilantro.

Italian Chicken

Sun-dried tomatoes and pesto are a winning combination in this dish.

Serves 4

2 tablespoons all-purpose flour

4 chicken portions (legs, breasts or
    quarters), skinned

2 tablespoons olive oil

1 onion, chopped

2 garlic cloves, chopped

1 red bell pepper, seeded and chopped

14-ounce can chopped tomatoes

2 tablespoons red pesto sauce

4 sun-dried tomatoes in oil, chopped

2/3 cup homemade or canned
    chicken stock

1 teaspoon dried oregano

8 black olives, pitted

salt and black pepper

chopped fresh basil and a few basil leaves,
    to garnish

tagliatelle, to serve

1 Place the flour and seasoning in a plastic bag. Add the chicken pieces and shake well until coated. Heat the oil in a flame-proof casserole, add the chicken and brown quickly. Remove with a spoon and set aside.

2 Lower the heat and add the onion, garlic and red pepper and cook for 5 minutes.

3 Stir in remaining ingredients, except the olives, and bring to a boil. Return the sautéed chicken to the casserole, season, cover and simmer for 30–35 minutes, or until the chicken is cooked.

4 Add the olives and simmer for 5 minutes. Place in a warmed serving dish, sprinkle with the chopped basil and garnish with a few basil leaves. Serve with hot tagliatelle, tossed in butter.

Honey and Orange Glazed Chicken

This way of cooking chicken breasts is popular in America, Australia and Great Britain. It is ideal for an easy evening meal served with baked potatoes and salad.

Serves 4

6 ounces boneless chicken breasts

1 tablespoon oil

4 scallions, chopped

1 garlic clove, crushed

3 tablespoons honey

4 tablespoons fresh orange juice

1 orange, peeled and segmented

2 tablespoons soy sauce

fresh lemon balm or flat leaf parsley, to
    garnish

baked potatoes and mixed salad, to serve

1 Preheat the oven to 375°F. Place the chicken breasts in a shallow roasting pan and set aside.

2 Heat the oil in a small pan, and fry the scallions and garlic for 2 minutes, until softened. Add the honey, orange juice, orange segments and soy sauce to the pan, stirring well until the honey has dissolved.

3 Pour the sauce over the chicken and bake, uncovered, for about 45 minutes, basting with the honey glaze once or twice, until the chicken is cooked. Garnish with the lemon balm or parsley and serve the chicken and its sauce with baked potatoes and a salad.

Louisiana Rice

A tasty meal of pork, rice, chicken livers and an array of spices.

INGREDIENTS

Serves 4

4 tablespoons vegetable oil
1 small eggplant, diced
8 ounces ground pork
1 green bell pepper, seeded and chopped
2 stalks celery, chopped
1 onion, chopped
1 garlic clove, crushed
1 teaspoon cayenne pepper
1 teaspoon paprika
1 teaspoon black pepper
$^1/_2$ teaspoon salt
1 teaspoon dried thyme
$^1/_2$ teaspoon dried oregano
2 cups homemade or canned
   chicken stock
8 ounces chicken livers, minced
$^3/_4$ cup long-grain rice
1 bay leaf
3 tablespoons chopped fresh parsley
celery leaves, to garnish

1 Heat the oil in a frying pan until really hot, then add the diced eggplant and stir-fry for about 5 minutes.

2 Add the pork and cook for about 6–8 minutes, until browned, using a wooden spoon to break any lumps.

3 Add the chopped green pepper, celery, onion, garlic and all the spices and herbs. Cover and cook over high heat for 5–6 minutes, stirring frequently from the bottom to scrape up and distribute the crispy brown bits.

4 Pour on the chicken stock and stir to clean the bottom of the pan. Cover and cook for 6 minutes over medium heat. Stir in the chicken livers, cook for 2 minutes, then stir in the rice and add the bay leaf.

5 Reduce the heat, cover and simmer for about 6–7 minutes. Turn off the heat and let stand for another 10–15 minutes, until the rice is tender. Remove the bay leaf and stir in the chopped parsley. Serve the rice hot, garnished with the celery leaves.

Chinese Special Fried Rice

Cooked white rice fried with a selection of other ingredients is a staple Chinese dish. This recipe combines a mixture of chicken, shrimp and vegetables with fried rice.

INGREDIENTS

Serves 4

1 cup long-grain white rice
3 tablespoons peanut oil
1 garlic clove, crushed
4 scallions, finely chopped
1 cup diced cooked chicken
1 cup cooked peeled shrimp
    (rinsed if canned)
$1/2$ cup frozen peas
1 egg, beaten with a pinch of salt
1 cup shredded lettuce
2 tablespoons light soy sauce
pinch of sugar
salt and black pepper
1 tablespoon chopped roasted cashews, to
    garnish

1 Rinse the long-grain rice in two to three changes of warm water to wash away some of the starch. Drain well.

2 Put the rice in a saucepan and add 1 tablespoon of the oil and $1^1/2$ cups of water. Cover and bring to a boil, stir once, then cover and simmer for 12–15 minutes, until nearly all the water has been absorbed. Turn off the heat and let stand covered for 10 minutes. Fluff rice with a fork and let cool, uncovered.

3 Heat the remaining oil in a wok or frying pan, add the garlic and scallions and stir-fry for 30 seconds.

4 Add the chicken, shrimp and peas and stir-fry for 1–2 minutes, then add the cooked rice and stir-fry for another 2 minutes. Pour in the egg and stir-fry until just set. Stir in the lettuce, soy sauce, sugar and seasoning.

5 Transfer to a warmed serving bowl, sprinkle with the chopped roasted cashews and serve immediately.

Chicken Teriyaki

Boiled rice is the ideal accompaniment to this Japanese-style dish.

Serves 4

1 pound chicken breasts, boned and
    skinned
orange segments, mustard greens and
    watercress, to garnish

For the marinade
1 teaspoon sugar
1 tablespoon rice wine
1 tablespoon dry sherry
2 tablespoons dark soy sauce
rind of 1 orange, grated

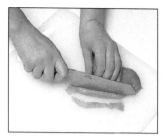

1 Slice the chicken breasts into thin strips. Mix all the marinade ingredients in a bowl.

2 Place the chicken in a bowl, pour on the marinade and let marinate for 15 minutes.

3 Heat a wok or large frying pan, add the chicken and marinade and stir-fry for 4–5 minutes. Serve the chicken garnished with orange segments and the greens.

COOK'S TIP

Make sure the marinade is brought to a boil and cooked for 4–5 minutes, because it has been in contact with raw chicken.

Thai Fried Noodles

Pork, chicken and fish stir-fried with noodles and lime juice.

INGREDIENTS

Serves 4

8 ounces thread egg noodles
4 tablespoons vegetable oil
2 garlic cloves, finely chopped
6 ounces pork tenderloin,
    sliced into thin strips
1 chicken breast, about 6 ounces, boned,
    skinned and sliced into thin strips
1 cup cooked peeled shrimps
    (rinsed if canned)
3 tablespoons lime or lemon juice
3 tablespoons Thai fish sauce
2 tablespoons light brown sugar
2 eggs, beaten
$1/2$ red chili, seeded and finely chopped
$1/4$ cup beansprouts
4 tablespoons roasted peanuts, chopped
3 scallions, cut into 2-inch lengths
    and shredded
3 tablespoons chopped fresh cilantro

1 Place the noodles in a large pan of boiling water and let stand for about 5 minutes.

2 Meanwhile, heat 3 tablespoons of the oil in a wok or large frying pan, add the garlic and cook for 30 seconds. Add the pork and chicken and stir-fry over high heat until lightly browned, then add the shrimp, and stir-fry for 2 minutes.

3 Add the lime or lemon juice, fish sauce and sugar and stir-fry until the sugar has dissolved.

4 Drain the noodles and add to the pan with the remaining 1 tablespoon oil. Toss all the ingredients together.

5 Pour on the beaten eggs. Stir-fry until almost set, then add the chili and beansprouts. Divide the peanuts, scallions and cilantro leaves into two and add half to the pan. Stir-fry for 2 minutes, then tip on to a serving platter. Sprinkle on the remaining peanuts, scallions and cilantro and serve at once.

Chicken and Shrimp Jambalaya

The mixture of chicken, seafood and rice suggests a close relationship to the Spanish paella, but the name is probably derived from jambon (French for ham) and à la ya (Creole for rice). Jambalayas are a colorful mixture of highly flavored ingredients, and are always made in large quantities for big family or celebration meals.

INGREDIENTS

Serves 10

2 chickens, 3 pounds each

1 pound piece raw smoked ham

4 tablespoons crisco or bacon fat

1/2 cup all-purpose flour

3 medium onions, finely sliced

2 green bell peppers,
   seeded and sliced

1 1/2 pounds tomatoes, skinned and
   chopped

2–3 garlic cloves, crushed

2 teaspoons chopped fresh thyme
   or 1 teaspoon dried thyme

24 cooked large shrimp, heads removed
   and peeled

3 cups long-grain rice

2–3 dashes Tabasco sauce

1 bunch scallions, finely chopped
   (including the green parts)

3 tablespoons chopped fresh parsley

salt and black pepper

COOK'S TIP

The roux thickening is a vital part of Cajun cooking, particularly essential to jambalaya. Cook the roux over low heat, watching like a hawk so that it doesn't develop dark flecks, which indicate burning. Don't stop stirring for an instant.

1 Cut each chicken into 10 pieces and season with salt and pepper.

2 Dice the ham, discarding the rind and fat.

3 In a large heavy-bottomed pan melt the lard or bacon fat and brown the chicken pieces all over, lifting them out with a slotted spoon and setting them aside as they are done.

4 Turn the heat down, sprinkle the flour onto the fat in the pan and stir continuously until the roux turns light golden brown (see Cook's Tip below).

5 Return the chicken pieces to the pan, add the diced ham, onions, green peppers, tomatoes, garlic and thyme and cook, stirring often, for 10 minutes, then stir in the shrimp.

6 Stir the rice into the pan with one-and-a-half times the rice's volume in cold water. Season with salt, pepper and Tabasco sauce. Bring to a boil and cook over gentle heat until the rice is tender and the liquid absorbed. Add a little extra boiling water if the rice looks like it is drying out before it is cooked.

7 Mix the scallions and parsley into the finished dish, reserving a little of the mixture to sprinkle over the jambalaya as a garnish. Serve hot.

Burgundy Chicken

A dinner-party classic, perfect with a good bottle of red wine.

INGREDIENTS

Serves 4

4 tablespoons all-purpose flour
1 chicken, 3 pounds, cut into 8 pieces
1 tablespoon olive oil
5 tablespoons butter
20 baby onions
3 ounces piece lean bacon without
    rind, diced
about 20 button mushrooms
1 bottle red Burgundy wine
bouquet garni
3 garlic cloves
1 teaspoon light brown sugar
salt and black pepper
1 tablespoon chopped fresh parsley and
    croutons, to garnish

1 Place 3 tablespoons of the flour and the seasoning in a large plastic bag and shake each chicken piece in it until lightly coated. Heat the oil and 4 tablespoons of the butter in a large flameproof casserole. Add the onions and bacon and sauté for 3–4 minutes, until the onions have lightly browned. Add the mushrooms and fry for 2 minutes. Remove with a slotted spoon into a bowl and reserve.

2 Add the chicken pieces to the hot oil and cook until browned on all sides, about 5–6 minutes. Pour on the Burgundy wine and add the bouquet garni, garlic, light brown sugar and seasoning.

3 Bring to a boil, cover and simmer for 1 hour, stirring occasionally.

4 Return the reserved onions, bacon and mushrooms to the casserole, cover and cook for another 30 minutes.

5 Lift out the cooked chicken, vegetables and bacon with a slotted spoon and arrange on a warmed dish. Remove the bouquet garni and boil the liquid rapidly for 2 minutes to reduce slightly. Cream the remaining butter and flour together and whisk in teaspoonfuls of the mixture until thickened slightly. Pour over the chicken and garnish with parsley and croutons.

Apricot and Chicken Casserole

A mild curried and fruity chicken dish served with almond rice. Makes a good winter meal.

Serves 4

1 tablespoon oil
8 chicken thighs, boned and skinned
1 medium onion, finely chopped
1 teaspoon medium curry powder
2 tablespoons all-purpose flour
1 7/8 cups homemade or canned
    chicken stock
juice of 1 large orange
8 dried apricots, halved
1 tablespoon golden raisins
salt and black pepper

For the almond rice

2 cups cooked long-grain rice
1 tablespoon butter
1/2 cup toasted, slivered almonds

3 Add the apricots and golden raisins, cover with a lid and cook gently for an hour, or until tender, in the preheated oven. Adjust the seasoning to taste.

4 To make the almond rice, reheat the pre-cooked rice with the butter and season to taste. Stir in the toasted almonds just before serving.

1 Preheat the oven to 375°F. Heat the oil in a large frying pan. Cut the chicken into cubes and brown quickly all over in the oil. Add the chopped onion and cook gently until soft and lightly browned.

2 Transfer the chicken and onion to a large flameproof casserole, sprinkle in the curry powder and cook again for a few minutes. Add the flour and blend in the stock and orange juice. Bring to a boil and season with salt and freshly ground black pepper.

Chicken in Creamed Horseradish

The piquant flavor of horseradish sauce gives this quick dish a sophisticated taste. Use half the quantity if using fresh horseradish.

Serves 4

2 tablespoons olive oil

4 chicken pieces

2 tablespoons butter

2 tablespoons all-purpose flour

$1^{7}/_{8}$ cups homemade or canned chicken stock

2 tablespoons bottled horseradish sauce

salt and black pepper

1 tablespoon chopped fresh parsley, to garnish

mashed potatoes and tender green beans, to serve

1 Heat the oil in a large flame-proof casserole and gently brown the chicken pieces on both sides over medium heat. Remove the chicken from the casserole and keep warm.

2 Wipe out the casserole, melt the butter, stir in the flour and blend in the stock gradually. Bring to a boil, stirring all the time.

3 Add the horseradish sauce and season with salt and freshly ground black pepper. Return the chicken to the casserole, cover and simmer for 30–40 minutes, or until the chicken is tender.

4 Transfer to a serving dish and sprinkle with fresh parsley. Serve with mashed potatoes and green beans, if desired.

Chicken Paella

There are many variations of this basic recipe. Any seasonal vegetables can be added, together with mussels and other shellfish. Serve right from the pan.

INGREDIENTS

Serves 4

4 chicken legs (thighs and drumsticks)
4 tablespoons olive oil
1 large onion, finely chopped
1 garlic clove, crushed
1 teaspoon ground turmeric
4 ounces chorizo sausage or smoked ham
1 cup long-grain rice
2 1/2 cups homemade or canned
   chicken stock
4 tomatoes, skinned, seeded and chopped
1 red bell pepper, seeded and sliced
1 cup frozen peas
salt and black pepper

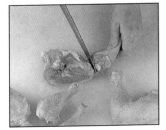

1 Preheat the oven to 350°F. Cut the chicken legs in half.

2 Heat the oil in a 12-inch paella pan or large flameproof casserole and brown the chicken pieces on both sides. Add the onion and garlic and stir in the turmeric. Cook for 2 minutes.

3 Slice the sausage or dice the ham and add to the pan, with the rice and stock. Bring to a boil and season to taste; cover and bake for 15 minutes.

4 Remove from the oven and add the chopped tomatoes, sliced red pepper and frozen peas. Return to the oven and cook for another 10–15 minutes, or until the chicken is tender and the rice has absorbed the stock.

Chicken with Bell Peppers

This colorful dish comes from the south of Italy, where sweet peppers are plentiful.

INGREDIENTS

Serves 4

1 chicken, 3 pounds, cut into
    serving pieces
3 large bell peppers, red, yellow or green
6 tablespoons olive oil
2 medium red onions, finely sliced
2 cloves garlic, finely chopped
small piece of dried chili, crumbled
    (optional)
$^1/_2$ cup white wine
salt and black pepper
2 tomatoes, fresh or canned, peeled and
    chopped
3 tablespoons chopped fresh parsley

1 Trim any fat off the chicken, and remove all excess skin. Prepare peppers by cutting them in half and discarding the seeds and the stem. Slice into strips.

2 Heat half the oil in a large heavy saucepan or casserole. Add the onions, and cook over low heat until soft. Remove to a side dish. Add the remaining oil to the pan, raise the heat to medium, add the chicken and brown on all sides, 6–8 minutes. Return the onions to the pan, and add the garlic and dried chili, if using.

3 Pour in the wine, and cook until it has reduced by half. Add the peppers and stir well to coat them with the oil. Season. After 3–4 minutes, stir in the tomatoes. Lower the heat, cover the pan, and cook until the peppers are soft, and the chicken is cooked, about 25–30 minutes. Stir occasionally. Stir in the chopped parsley and serve.

Chicken Breasts Cooked in Butter

This simple and very delicious way of cooking chicken brings out all of its delicacy.

INGREDIENTS

Serves 4

4 small chicken breasts, skinned
    and boned
flour seasoned with salt and freshly
    ground black pepper, for dredging
6 tablespoons butter
1 sprig fresh parsley, to garnish

1 Separate the two fillets of each breast. They come apart very easily; one is large, the other small. Pound the large fillets between two sheets of plastic wrap lightly to flatten them. Dredge the chicken in the seasoned flour, shaking off any excess.

2 Heat the butter in a large heavy frying pan until it bubbles. Place all the chicken fillets in the pan, in one layer if possible. Cook over medium to high heat for 3–4 minutes, until they are golden brown.

3 Turn the chicken over. Reduce the heat to low to medium, and continue cooking until the fillets are cooked through but still springy to the touch, about 9–12 minutes in all. If the chicken begins to brown too much, cover the pan for the final minutes of cooking. Serve immediately garnished with a little parsley.

Chicken in Green Sauce

Slow, gentle cooking makes the chicken succulent and tender.

INGREDIENTS

Serves 4

2 tablespoons butter
1 tablespoon olive oil
4 chicken portions
1 small onion, finely chopped
²/₃ cup medium dry white wine
²/₃ cup homemade or canned
   chicken stock
6 ounces watercress
2 thyme sprigs and 2 tarragon sprigs
²/₃ cup heavy cream
salt and black pepper
watercress leaves, to garnish

1 Heat the butter and oil in a heavy shallow pan, then brown the chicken evenly. Transfer the chicken to a plate, using a slotted spoon, and keep warm in the oven.

2 Add the onion to the cooking juices in the pan and cook until softened but not colored.

3 Stir in the wine, boil for 2–3 minutes, then add the stock and bring to a boil. Return the chicken to the pan, cover tightly and cook very gently for about 30 minutes, until the chicken juices run clear. Then transfer the chicken to a warm dish, cover the dish and keep warm.

4 Boil the cooking juices hard until reduced to about 4 tablespoons. Add the leaves from the watercress and herbs to the pan with the cream and simmer over medium heat until the sauce has thickened slightly.

5 Return the cooked chicken to the casserole, season and heat through for a few minutes. Garnish with watercress leaves before serving.

Stoved Chicken

"Stoved" is derived from the French étouffer – to cook in a covered pot – and originates from the seventeenth century.

Serves 4

2$\frac{1}{4}$ pounds potatoes,
    cut into $\frac{1}{4}$-inch slices
2 large onions, thinly sliced
1 tablespoon chopped fresh thyme
2 tablespoons butter
1 tablespoon oil
2 large slices bacon, chopped
4 large chicken quarters, halved
1 bay leaf
2$\frac{1}{2}$ cups homemade or canned
    chicken stock
salt and black pepper

1 Preheat the oven to 300°F. Make a thick layer of half the potato slices in the bottom of a large, heavy casserole, then cover with half the onion. Sprinkle with half the thyme, and salt and pepper.

2 Heat the butter and oil in a large frying pan, then brown the bacon and chicken.

3 Using a slotted spoon, transfer the chicken and bacon to the casserole. Reserve the fat in the pan. Sprinkle the remaining thyme, bay leaf and some seasoning over the chicken, then cover with the remaining onion, followed by a neat layer of overlapping potato slices. Sprinkle with seasoning.

4 Pour the stock into the casserole, brush the potatoes with the reserved fat, then cover tightly and cook in the oven for about 2 hours, until the chicken is tender.

5 Preheat the broiler. Uncover the casserole, place under the broiler and cook until the slices of potato are beginning to brown and crisp. Serve hot.

Parmesan Chicken Bake

The tomato sauce may be made the day before and left to cool. Serve with crusty bread and salad.

INGREDIENTS

Serves 4

4 chicken breasts, boned and skinned
4 tablespoons all-purpose flour
4 tablespoons olive oil
salt and black pepper

For the tomato sauce

1 tablespoon olive oil
1 onion, finely chopped
1 stalk celery, finely chopped
1 red bell pepper, seeded and diced
1 garlic clove, crushed
14-ounce can chopped tomatoes with
    their juice
$^2/_3$ cup homemade/canned chicken stock
1 tablespoon tomato paste
2 teaspoons sugar
1 tablespoon chopped fresh basil
1 tablespoon chopped fresh parsley

To assemble

8 ounces mozzarella cheese, sliced
4 tablespoons grated Parmesan cheese
2 tablespoons fresh breadcrumbs

1 To make the tomato sauce, heat 1 tablespoon of the oil in a frying pan and gently cook the onion, celery, pepper and crushed garlic in the oil until tender.

2 Add the tomatoes with their juice, the stock, paste, sugar and herbs. Season to taste and bring to a boil. Simmer for 30 minutes to make a thick sauce, stirring occasionally.

3 Divide the chicken breasts into two natural fillets, place between sheets of plastic wrap and flatten to a thickness of $^1/_4$ inch with a rolling pin.

4 Season the flour. Toss the chicken breasts in the flour to coat, shaking to remove the excess.

5 Preheat the oven to 350°F. Heat the remaining oil in a large frying pan and cook the chicken quickly in batches for 3–4 minutes, until colored. Remove and keep warm while frying the rest of the chicken.

6 To assemble, layer the chicken pieces in a large baking dish with the cheeses and thick tomato sauce, finishing with a layer of cheese and breadcrumbs on top. Bake uncovered for 20–30 minutes or until golden brown.

Chicken with Mushrooms

Serve on a dish surrounded with nutty brown rice or tagliatelle verde. White wine or brandy may be used to deglaze the pan in place of sherry.

INGREDIENTS

Serves 4

4 large chicken breasts, boned and skinned
3 tablespoons olive oil
1 onion, thinly sliced
1 garlic clove, crushed
3 cups button mushrooms,
   quartered
2 tablespoons sherry
1 tablespoon lemon juice
1/3 cup light cream
salt and black pepper

3 Add the mushrooms and cook them for another 5 minutes. Remove and keep warm.

4 Increase the heat. Add the remaining oil and fry the chicken very quickly, in small batches, for 3–4 minutes, until lightly colored. Season each batch with a little salt and freshly ground black pepper. Remove and keep warm on a plate while frying the rest of the chicken.

5 Add the sherry and lemon juice to the pan and quickly return the chicken, onions, garlic and mushrooms, stirring to coat.

6 Stir in the cream and bring to a boil. Adjust the seasoning to taste. Serve immediately.

1 Divide the chicken breasts into two natural fillets. Place each between two sheets of plastic wrap and flatten to a thickness of 1/4 inch with a rolling pin. Cut into 1-inch diagonal strips.

2 Heat 2 tablespoons of the oil in a large frying pan and cook the onion and crushed garlic slowly until tender.

Chicken with White Wine and Garlic

Add the extra garlic to this dish if you like a stronger flavor.

INGREDIENTS

Serves 4

1 chicken, 3¹/2 pounds,
   cut into serving pieces
1 onion, sliced
3–6 garlic cloves, to taste, crushed
1 teaspoon dried thyme
2 cups dry white wine
1 cup green olives (16–18),
   pitted
1 bay leaf
1 tablespoon lemon juice
1–2 tablespoons butter
salt and black pepper

1 Heat a deep, heavy frying pan. When hot, add the chicken pieces, skin side down, and cook over medium heat until browned, about 10 minutes. Turn and brown the other side, 5–8 minutes more.

2 Transfer the chicken pieces to a plate and set aside.

3 Drain the excess fat from the frying pan, leaving about 1 tablespoon. Add the sliced onion and ¹/2 teaspoon salt and cook until just soft, about 5 minutes. Add the garlic and thyme and cook 1 minute more.

4 Add the wine and stir, scraping up any bits that cling to the pan. Bring to a boil and boil for 1 minute. Stir in the olives.

5 Return the chicken pieces to the pan. Add the bay leaf and season lightly with pepper. Lower the heat, cover, and simmer until the chicken is cooked through, about 20–30 minutes.

6 Transfer the chicken pieces to a warmed plate. Stir the lemon juice into the sauce. Whisk in the butter to thicken the sauce slightly. Spoon on top and serve.

Chicken Meat Loaf

Just slice the loaf up and serve it hot or cold.

INGREDIENTS

Serves 4

1 tablespoon olive oil
1 onion, chopped
1 green bell pepper, seeded and chopped
1 garlic clove, crushed
1 pound ground chicken
1 cup fresh breadcrumbs
1 egg, beaten
¹/2 cup pine nuts
12 sun-dried tomatoes in oil, drained and
   chopped
5 tablespoons milk
2 teaspoons chopped fresh rosemary, or
   ¹/2 teaspoon dried rosemary
1 teaspoon ground fennel seeds
¹/2 teaspoon dried oregano
¹/2 teaspoon salt

1 Preheat the oven to 375°F. Heat the oil in a frying pan. Add the onion, green pepper and garlic and cook over low heat, stirring often, until just softened, about 8–10 minutes. Remove from the heat and allow to cool.

2 Place the chicken in a large bowl. Add the onion mixture and the remaining ingredients and mix thoroughly.

3 Transfer to an 8¹/2 x 4¹/2-inch loaf tin, packing the mixture down firmly. Bake until golden brown, about 1 hour. Serve hot or cold in slices.

French-style Pot Roast Rock Cornish Hens

An incredibly simple dish that looks and tastes extra special.

Serves 4

1 tablespoon olive oil

1 onion, sliced

1 large garlic clove, sliced

1/2 cup diced lightly smoked bacon

2 fresh Rock Cornish hens, just under 1 pound each

2 tablespoons melted butter

2 baby celery hearts, each cut into 4 pieces

8 baby carrots

2 small zucchini, cut into chunk

8 small new potatoes

2 1/2 cups homemade or canned chicken stock

2/3 cup dry white wine

1 bay leaf

2 fresh thyme sprigs

2 fresh rosemary sprigs

1 tablespoon butter, softened

1 tablespoon all-purpose flour

salt and black pepper

fresh herbs, to garnish

1 Preheat the oven to 375°F. Heat the olive oil in a large flame-proof casserole and add the onion, garlic and bacon. Sauté for 5–6 minutes, until the onion has softened.

2 Brush the birds with a little melted butter and season well. Lay birds on top of the onion mixture with the vegetables around. Add the chicken stock, wine and herbs.

3 Cover, bake for 20 minutes, then remove the lid and brush the birds with the remaining melted butter. Bake for another 25–30 minutes, until golden.

4 Transfer the birds to a warmed serving platter and cut each in half with poultry shears or scissors. Remove the vegetables with a slotted spoon and arrange them around the birds. Cover with foil and keep warm.

5 Discard the herbs from the pan juices. In a bowl, mix the butter and flour to form a paste. Bring the liquid in the pan to a boil and then whisk in teaspoonfuls of the paste until thickened. Season the sauce and serve with the Rock Cornish hens and vegetables, garnished with fresh herbs.

Coq au Vin

There are many variations to this traditional French dish, but this one is especially delicious. Serve it with warm French bread.

Serves 4

2 tablespoons olive oil

2 tablespoons butter

1 chicken, 3^1/$_2$ pounds, cut into 8 pieces

4 ounces ham, cut into ^{1}/$_4$-inch strips

4 ounces baby onions, peeled

1^1/$_2$ cups button mushrooms

2 garlic cloves, crushed

2 tablespoons brandy

1 cup red wine

1^1/$_4$ cups homemade or canned
   chicken stock

1 bouquet garni

2 tablespoons butter, blended with
   2 tablespoons flour

salt and black pepper

chopped parsley, to garnish

1 Preheat the oven to 325°F. Heat the oil and butter in a large flameproof casserole and brown the chicken pieces on all sides.

2 Add the ham strips, peeled onions, mushrooms and crushed garlic.

3 Pour in the brandy and light it. When the flames have subsided, add the red wine, stock, bouquet garni and seasoning. Cover and cook slowly for about 1 hour in the preheated oven.

4 Remove the chicken and keep warm. Thicken the sauce with the butter mixture and season to taste. Cook for several minutes and replace the chicken. Sprinkle with chopped parsley and serve.

Chicken in Creamy Orange Sauce

This sauce is deceptively creamy – in fact, it is made with low-fat ricotta cheese, which is virtually fat-free. The brandy adds a rich flavor, but is optional – omit it if you wish and use orange juice alone.

INGREDIENTS

Serves 4

8 chicken thighs or drumsticks, skinned

3 tablespoons brandy

1¼ cups orange juice

3 scallions, chopped

2 teaspoons cornstarch

⅓ cup low-fat ricotta cheese

salt and black pepper

rice or pasta and green salad, to serve

1 Fry the chicken pieces without fat in a nonstick or heavy pan, turning until evenly browned.

2 Stir in the brandy, orange juice and scallions. Bring to a boil, then cover and simmer for 15 minutes, or until the chicken is tender and the juices run clear, not pink, when pierced.

3 Blend the cornstarch with a little water, then mix into the ricotta. Stir this into the sauce and stir over medium heat until boiling.

4 Adjust the seasoning and serve with boiled rice or pasta and green salad.

COOK'S TIP

Cornstarch helps to stabilize the ricotta cheese and stop it from curdling.

Tuscan Chicken

This simple peasant casserole has all the flavors of traditional Tuscan food. The wine can be replaced by chicken stock.

Serves 4

8 chicken thighs, skinned
1 teaspoon olive oil
1 medium onion, thinly sliced
2 red bell peppers, seeded and sliced
1 garlic clove, crushed
1¹/4 cups puréed tomatoes
²/3 cup dry white wine
large sprig fresh oregano, or 1 teaspoon
    dried oregano
14-ounce can cannellini beans, drained
3 tablespoons fresh breadcrumbs
salt and black pepper

1 Fry the chicken in the oil in a nonstick or heavy pan until golden brown. Remove and keep hot. Add the onion and peppers to the pan and gently sauté until softened, but not brown. Stir in the garlic.

2 Add the chicken, puréed tomatoes, wine and oregano. Season well, bring to a boil, then cover the pan tightly.

3 Lower the heat and simmer gently, stirring occasionally, for 30–35 minutes, or until the chicken is tender and the juices run clear, not pink, when pierced with the point of a knife.

4 Stir in the cannellini beans and simmer for another 5 minutes until heated through. Sprinkle with the breadcrumbs and cook under a hot broiler until golden brown.

Koftas in Tomato Sauce

Delicious meatballs in a rich tomato sauce. Serve with pasta and grated Parmesan cheese, if desired.

INGREDIENTS

Serves 4

1¹/2 pounds chicken
1 onion, grated
1 garlic clove, crushed
1 tablespoon chopped fresh parsley
¹/2 teaspoon ground cumin
¹/2 teaspoon ground coriander
1 egg, beaten
seasoned flour, for rolling
¹/4 cup olive oil
salt and black pepper
chopped fresh parsley, to garnish

For the tomato sauce
1 tablespoon butter
2 tablespoons all-purpose flour
1 cup homemade or canned chicken stock
14-ounce can chopped tomatoes, with
  their juice
1 teaspoon sugar
¹/4 teaspoon dried mixed herbs

1 Preheat the oven to 350°F. Remove any skin and bone from the chicken and grind or chop finely.

2 Put into a bowl together with the onion, garlic, parsley, spices, seasoning and beaten egg.

3 Mix thoroughly and shape into 1¹/2-inch balls. Roll lightly in seasoned flour.

4 Heat the oil in a frying pan and brown the balls in small batches (this keeps the oil temperature hot and prevents the flour from becoming soggy). Remove and drain on paper towels. There is no need to cook the balls any longer at this stage, as they will cook in the tomato sauce.

5 To make the tomato sauce, melt the butter in a large saucepan. Add the flour, and then blend in the stock and tomatoes along with their juice. Add the sugar and mixed herbs. Bring to a boil, cover and simmer for 10–15 minutes.

6 Place the browned chicken balls into a shallow ovenproof dish and pour on the tomato sauce, cover with foil and bake in the preheated oven for 30–40 minutes. Adjust the seasoning to taste and sprinkle with parsley.

Spanish Chicken

*A colorful one pot dish, ideal for
entertaining and delicious served
with a crisp green salad.*

INGREDIENTS

Serves 8

2 tablespoons all-purpose flour

2 teaspoons ground paprika

$^1/_2$ teaspoon salt

16 chicken drumsticks

$^1/_4$ cup olive oil

5 cups homemade or canned
    chicken stock

1 onion, finely chopped

2 garlic cloves, crushed

$2^2/_3$ cups long-grain rice

2 bay leaves

$1^1/_3$ cups diced cooked ham

1 cup pimento-stuffed green olives

1 green bell pepper, seeded and diced

14-ounce cans chopped tomatoes, with
    their juice

4 tablespoons chopped fresh parsley

1 Preheat the oven to 350°F.
Shake together the flour,
paprika and salt in a plastic bag,
add the drumsticks and toss
to coat.

2 Heat the oil in a large flameproof casserole and, working in
batches, brown the chicken drumsticks slowly on all sides. Remove
and keep warm.

3 Meanwhile, bring the stock
to a boil and add the onion,
crushed garlic, rice and bay leaves.
Cook for 10 minutes. Add the
ham, olives, pepper, and canned
tomatoes with their juice. Mix well
and transfer to a shallow
ovenproof dish.

4 Arrange the chicken on top,
cover and bake for 30–40
minutes, or until tender. Add a
little more stock, if necessary, to
prevent it from drying out.
Remove the bay leaves and sprinkle
on the chopped parsley to garnish.

Chicken with Lemon and Herbs

The herbs can be changed according to what is available; for example, parsley or thyme could be used instead of tarragon and fennel.

INGREDIENTS

Serves 2

4 tablespoons butter
2 scallions, white part only, finely chopped
1 tablespoon chopped fresh tarragon
1 tablespoon chopped fresh fennel
juice of 1 lemon
4 chicken thighs
salt and black pepper
lemon slices and herb sprigs, to garnish

1 Preheat the broiler to medium. In a small saucepan, melt the butter, then add the scallions, herbs, lemon juice and seasoning.

2 Brush the chicken generously with the herb mixture, then broil for 10–12 minutes, basting frequently with the herb mixture.

3 Turn over and baste again, then cook for another 10–12 minutes, or until the chicken juices run clear.

4 Serve garnished with lemon and herbs and with any remaining herb mixture.

Chicken with Red Cabbage

Chestnuts and red cabbage make a colorful winter dish.

INGREDIENTS

Serves 4

4 tablespoons butter
4 large chicken portions, halved
1 onion, chopped
1 1/4 pounds red cabbage, finely shredded
4 juniper berries, crushed
12 cooked peeled chestnuts
1/2 cup full-bodied red wine
salt and black pepper

1 Heat the butter in a heavy flameproof casserole and lightly brown the chicken pieces. Transfer to a plate.

2 Add the onion to the casserole and fry gently until soft and light golden brown. Stir the cabbage and juniper berries into the casserole, season and cook over medium heat for 6–7 minutes, stirring once or twice.

3 Stir the chestnuts into the casserole, then tuck the chicken pieces under the cabbage so they are on the bottom of the casserole. Pour in the red wine.

4 Cover and cook gently for about 40 minutes, until the chicken juices run clear and the cabbage is very tender. Check the seasoning and serve.

Chicken with Blackberries and Lemon

This delicious stew combines some wonderful flavors. The red wine and blackberries give it a dramatic appearance.

INGREDIENTS

Serves 4

4 partly boned chicken breasts
2 tablespoons butter
1 tablespoon sunflower oil
4 tablespoons all-purpose flour
$^2/_3$ cup red wine
$^2/_3$ cup homemade or canned
    chicken stock
grated rind of $^1/_2$ orange,
    plus 1 tablespoon juice
3 sprigs lemon balm, finely chopped, plus
    1 sprig to garnish
$^2/_3$ cup heavy cream
1 egg yolk
1 cup fresh blackberries,
    plus $^1/_2$ cup to garnish
salt and black pepper

1 Preheat the oven to 350°F. Remove any skin from the chicken, and season the meat. Heat the butter and oil in a frying pan, fry the chicken until golden, then transfer to a casserole dish. Stir the flour into the pan, then add the wine and stock and bring to a boil. Add the orange rind and juice, and the chopped lemon balm. Pour over the chicken.

2 Cover the casserole and cook in the oven for about 40 minutes.

3 Blend the cream with the egg yolk, add some of the liquid from the casserole and stir back into the dish with the blackberries (reserving those for the garnish). Cover and cook for another 10–15 minutes. Serve garnished with the rest of the blackberries and the sprig of lemon balm.

Chicken with Cajun Sauce

*Sizzling fried chicken served in a
tasty tomato sauce.*

Serves 4

1 chicken, 3^1/2 pounds, cut into 8 pieces
^{3}/4 cup all-purpose flour
1 cup buttermilk or milk
vegetable oil, for frying
salt and black pepper
chopped scallions, to garnish

For the sauce
^{2}/3 cup crisco or vegetable oil
9 tablespoons all-purpose flour
2 onions, chopped
2–3 celery stalks, chopped
1 large green bell pepper, seeded
    and chopped
2 garlic cloves, finely chopped
1 cup puréed tomatoes
1^7/8 cups red wine or homemade
    or canned chicken stock
1^3/4 cups tomatoes, skinned
    and chopped
2 bay leaves
1 tablespoon brown sugar
1 teaspoon grated orange rind
^{1}/2 teaspoon cayenne pepper

1 To make the sauce, heat the
lard or oil in a large, heavy pan
and stir in the flour. Cook over
medium low heat, stirring
constantly, for 15–20 minutes, or
until the mixture has darkened to
the color of hazelnut shells.

2 Add the chopped onions,
celery, green pepper and garlic
and cook, stirring, until the
vegetables are softened.

3 Stir in the remaining sauce
ingredients with salt and
pepper to taste. Bring to a boil,
then simmer for 1 hour, or until
the sauce is rich and thick. Stir
occasionally.

4 Meanwhile, prepare the
chicken. Put the flour in a
plastic bag and season with salt
and pepper. Dip each piece of
chicken in buttermilk, then dredge
in the flour to coat lightly all over.
Shake off excess flour. Set the
chicken aside for 20 minutes to let
the coating set before frying.

5 Heat the vegetable oil 1 inch
deep in a large frying pan
until it is very hot and starting to
sizzle. Fry the chicken pieces,
turning them once, for about
30 minutes or until deep golden
brown all over and cooked
through.

6 Drain the chicken pieces on
paper towels. Add them to the
sauce and sprinkle with chopped
scallions.

Pot Roast Chicken with Sausage Stuffing

These casseroled chickens will be tender and succulent.

Serves 6

2 chickens, 2¹/₂ pounds each
2 tablespoons vegetable oil
1¹/₂ cups homemade or canned chicken
    stock or half wine and half stock
1 bay leaf

For the stuffing
1 pound sausage
1 small onion, chopped
1–2 garlic cloves, finely chopped
1 teaspoon hot paprika
¹/₂ teaspoon dried chili
    (optional)
¹/₂ teaspoon dried thyme
¹/₄ teaspoon ground allspice
1 cup coarse fresh breadcrumbs
1 egg, beaten to mix
salt and black pepper

1 Preheat the oven to 350°F.

2 For the stuffing, put the sausage, onion and garlic in a frying pan and fry over medium heat until the sausage is lightly browned and crumbly, stirring and turning so it cooks evenly. Remove from the heat and mix in the remaining stuffing ingredients with salt and pepper to taste.

3 Divide the stuffing between the chickens, packing it into the body cavities (or, if preferred, stuff the neck end and bake the leftover stuffing in a separate dish). Truss the birds.

4 Heat the oil in a flameproof casserole just big enough to hold the chickens. Brown the birds all over.

5 Add the stock and bay leaf and season. Cover and bring to a boil, then transfer to the oven. Roast, covered, for 1¹/₄ hours or until the birds are cooked (the juices will run clear).

6 Untruss the chickens and spoon the stuffing onto a serving platter. Arrange the birds and serve with the strained cooking liquid.

VARIATION

For Pot Roast Guinea Hens, use 2 guinea hens instead of chickens.

Rock Cornish Hens Waldorf

Sunday roast and stuffing, with a difference.

INGREDIENTS

Serves 6

6 Rock Cornish hens, about
  1^1/$_4$ pounds each
salt and black pepper
3–4 tablespoons butter or margarine
  melted

For the stuffing
2 tablespoons butter
1 onion, finely chopped
2^1/$_4$ cups cooked rice
2 celery stalks, finely chopped
2 red apples, cored and finely diced
^{1}/$_3$ cup walnuts, chopped
5 tablespoons cream sherry or apple juice
2 tablespoons lemon juice

1 Preheat the oven to 350°F. To make the stuffing, melt the butter in a small frying pan and fry the onion, stirring occasionally, until soft. Pour the onion and butter into a bowl and add the remaining stuffing ingredients. Season with salt and pepper and mix well.

2 Divide the stuffing among the birds, stuffing the body cavities. Truss the birds and arrange in a roasting pan. Sprinkle with salt and pepper and drizzle on the melted butter.

3 Roast for about 1^1/$_4$–1^1/$_2$ hours. Untruss before serving.

CARVING POULTRY

Carving a bird neatly for serving makes the presentation attractive. You will need a sharp long-bladed knife, or an electric knife, plus a long 2-pronged fork and a carving board with a groove around the border to catch the juices.

Cut away any trussing string. For a stuffed bird, spoon the stuffing from the cavity into a serving dish. For easier carving, remove the wishbone.

Insert the fork into one breast to hold the bird steady. Cut through the skin to the ball and socket joint on that side of the body, then slice through it to sever the leg from the body. Repeat on the other side.

1 Slice through the ball and socket joint in each leg to sever the thigh and drumstick. If carving turkey, slice the meat off the thigh and drumstick, parallel to the bone, turning to get even slices; leave chicken thighs and drumsticks whole.

2 To carve the breast of a turkey or chicken, cut ^{1}/$_4$-inch thick slices at an angle, slicing down on both sides of the breastbone. For smaller birds, remove the meat on each side of the breastbone in a single piece, then slice across.

Chicken Brunswick Stew

This is chicken stew with a spicy bite, warming and filling.

INGREDIENTS

Serves 6

4 pounds chicken, cut in
    serving pieces
paprika
2 tablespoons olive oil
2 tablespoons butter
2 cups chopped onions
1 cup chopped green or yellow
    bell peppers
2 cups chopped peeled fresh or canned
    plum tomatoes
1 cup white wine
2 cups chicken homemade or canned
    stock or water
$^1/_4$ cup chopped fresh parsley
$^1/_2$ teaspoon hot pepper sauce
1 tablespoon Worcestershire sauce
2 cups corn (fresh, frozen
    or canned)
1 cup lima beans (fresh or frozen)
3 tablespoons all-purpose flour
salt and black pepper
rolls, rice, or potatoes, for serving
    (optional)

1 Pat the chicken pieces dry, then sprinkle them lightly with salt and paprika.

2 In a large heavy saucepan, heat the olive oil with the butter over medium-high heat. Heat until the mixture is sizzling and just starting to change color.

3 Add the chicken pieces and fry until golden brown on all sides. Remove the chicken pieces with tongs and set aside.

4 Reduce the heat to low and add the chopped onions and peppers to the pan. Cook until softened, 8–10 minutes.

5 Raise the heat. Add the tomatoes and their juice, the wine, stock or water, parsley, and hot pepper and Worcestershire sauces. Stir and bring to a boil.

6 Return the fried chicken pieces to the pan, pushing them down in the sauce. Cover, reduce the heat, and simmer 30 minutes, stirring occasionally.

7 Add the corn and lima beans and mix well. Partly cover and cook 30 minutes more.

8 Tilt the pan and skim off as much of the surface fat as possible. In a small bowl, mix the flour with a little water to make a paste.

9 Gradually stir in about $^3/_4$ cup of the hot sauce from the pan. Stir the flour mixture into the stew, and mix well to distribute it evenly and to thicken the stew. Cook 5–8 minutes more, stirring occasionally.

10 Check the seasoning. Serve the stew in shallow soup plates or large bowls.

Chicken with Sage, Prunes and Brandy

This stir-fry has a very rich sauce based on a good brandy – use the best you can afford.

Serves 4

4 ounces prunes

3–3¹/₂ pounds boneless chicken
  breast

1¹/₄ cups cognac or brandy

1 tablespoon fresh sage, chopped

5 ounces smoked bacon, in one piece

4 tablespoons butter

24 baby onions, peeled and quartered

salt and black pepper

fresh sage sprigs, to garnish

1 Pit the prunes and cut them into slivers. Remove the skin from the chicken and cut the breast into thin pieces.

2 Mix together the prunes, chicken, cognac and chopped sage in a non-metallic dish. Cover and let marinate overnight.

3 Next day, strain the chicken and prunes, reserving the cognac marinade mixture, and pat dry on paper towels.

4 Cut the smoked bacon into dice and set aside. Heat a wok or large frying pan and add half the butter. When the butter has melted, add the onions and stir-fry for 4 minutes, until crisp and golden. Then set aside.

5 Add the bacon to the wok and stir-fry for 1 minute, until it begins to release some fat. Add the remaining butter and stir-fry the chicken and prunes for 3–4 minutes, until crisp and golden. Push the chicken mixture to one side in the wok, add the cognac and simmer until thickened. Stir the chicken into the sauce, season well with salt and pepper, and serve garnished with sage.

Pasta Sauce with Chicken and Tomato

Perfect for a speedy supper – serve this with a mixed bean salad.

INGREDIENTS

Serves 4

1 tablespoon olive oil

1 onion, chopped

1 carrot, chopped

1 cup sun-dried tomatoes in olive oil

1 garlic clove, chopped

14-ounce can chopped tomatoes, drained

1 tablespoon tomato paste

$2/3$ cup homemade or canned
   chicken stock

3 cups pasta spirals (fusilli)

8 ounces chicken, diagonally sliced

salt and black pepper

sprigs fresh mint, to garnish

1 Heat the oil in a large frying pan and fry the chopped onion and carrot for 5 minutes, stirring occasionally.

2 Chop the sun-dried tomatoes and set aside.

3 Stir the garlic, canned tomatoes, tomato paste and stock into the onions and carrots and bring to a boil. Simmer for 10 minutes, stirring occasionally.

4 Cook the pasta in plenty of water, following the instructions on the package.

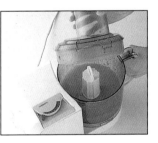

5 Pour the sauce into a food processor or blender and process until smooth.

COOK'S TIP

Sun-dried tomatoes are sold soaked in vegetable or olive oil in jars. The olive oil-soaked tomatoes have a superior flavor. For extra flavor, fry the onion and carrot in 1 tablespoon of the oil from the tomatoes.

6 Return the sauce to the pan and stir in the sun-dried tomatoes and chicken. Bring back to a boil, then simmer for 10 minutes until the chicken is cooked. Adjust the seasoning.

7 Drain the pasta thoroughly and toss it with the sauce. Serve immediately, garnished with sprigs of fresh mint.

Chicken with Sloe Gin and Juniper

Juniper is used in the manufacture of gin, and the reinforcement of the flavor by using both sloe gin and juniper is delicious. Sloe gin is easy to make, but can also be bought ready-made.

INGREDIENTS

Serves 8

2 tablespoons butter

2 tablespoons sunflower oil

8 chicken breast fillets

12 ounces carrots, cooked

1 clove garlic, crushed

1 tablespoon finely chopped parsley

$1/4$ cup homemade or canned
  chicken stock

$1/4$ cup red wine

$1/4$ cup sloe gin

1 teaspoon crushed juniper berries

salt and black pepper

chopped fresh basil, to garnish

1 Melt the butter with the oil in a frying pan, and fry the chicken until browned on all sides.

2 In a food processor or blender, combine all the remaining ingredients except the basil, and blend to a smooth paste. If the mixture seems too thick, add a little more red wine or water.

3 Put the chicken fillets in a clean pan, pour the sauce on top and cook over medium heat until the chicken is cooked through – about 15 minutes. Adjust the seasoning and serve garnished with chopped fresh basil.

Chicken with Figs and Mint

Refreshing mint and orange flavors go well with chicken.

INGREDIENTS

Serves 4

3 1/3 cups dried figs

1/2 bottle sweet, fruity white wine

4 boneless chicken breasts, about
   6–8 ounces each

1 tablespoon butter

2 tablespoons dark orange marmalade

10 mint leaves, finely chopped, plus a few
   more to garnish

juice of 1/2 lemon

salt and black pepper

1 Place the figs in a pan with the wine and bring to a boil, then simmer very gently for about 1 hour. Let cool and refrigerate overnight.

2 Fry the chicken breasts in the butter until they are cooked. Remove and keep warm. Drain any fat from the pan and pour in the juice from the figs. Boil and reduce to about 2/3 cup.

3 Add the marmalade, chopped mint leaves and lemon juice, and simmer for a few minutes. Season to taste. When the sauce is thick and shiny, pour it on the chicken, garnish with the figs and mint leaves and serve.

Chicken with Sauce Piquant

Sauce Piquant goes with everything that runs, flies or swims in Louisiana – you will even find Alligator with Sauce Piquant on menus. It is based on the brown Cajun roux, and chili peppers give it heat; vary the number you use.

INGREDIENTS

Serves 4

4 chicken legs or 2 legs and 2 breasts
$^{1}/_{3}$ cup cooking oil
$^{1}/_{2}$ cup all-purpose flour
1 medium onion, chopped
2 celery stalks, sliced
1 green bell pepper, seeded and diced
2 garlic cloves, crushed
1 bay leaf
$^{1}/_{2}$ teaspoon dried thyme
$^{1}/_{2}$ teaspoon dried oregano
1–2 red chili peppers, seeded and finely
  chopped
14-ounce can tomatoes, chopped, with
  their juice
$1^{1}/_{4}$ cups homemade or canned
  chicken stock
salt and black pepper
watercress to garnish
boiled potatoes to serve

1 Halve the chicken legs through the joint, or the breasts across the middle, to make 8 pieces.

2 In a heavy frying pan, fry the chicken pieces in the oil until brown on all sides, setting them aside as they are done.

3 Strain the oil from the pan into a heavy flameproof casserole. Heat it and stir in the flour. Stir constantly over a low heat until the roux is the color of peanut butter.

4 As soon as the roux reaches the right stage, add the onion, celery and pepper and stir over the heat for 2–3 minutes.

5 Add the garlic, bay leaf, thyme, oregano and chili pepper(s). Stir for 1 minute, then turn down the heat and stir in the tomatoes with their juice.

6 Return the casserole to the heat and gradually stir in the stock. Add the chicken pieces, cover and let simmer for 45 minutes, or until the chicken is tender.

7 If there is too much sauce or if it looks too runny, remove the lid for the last 10–15 minutes of the cooking time and turn up the heat a little.

8 Check the seasoning and serve, garnished with watercress and accompanied by boiled potatoes.

COOK'S TIP

If you prefer to err on the side of caution with chili heat, use just 1 chili pepper and heat up the seasoning at the end with a dash or two of Tabasco sauce. The oil in chili peppers clings to your skin and could hurt if you then rub your eyes. Scrape out the seeds under cold running water and wash your hands after handling chilies.

Stuffed Chicken Wings

These tasty stuffed wings can be served hot or cold at a buffet. They can be prepared and frozen in advance.

INGREDIENTS

Makes 12
12 large chicken wings

For the filling
1 teaspoon cornstarch
$^{1}/_{4}$ teaspoon salt
$^{1}/_{2}$ teaspoon fresh thyme
pinch of black pepper

For the coating
3 cups dried breadcrumbs
2 tablespoons sesame seeds
2 eggs, beaten
oil, for deep-frying

1 Remove the wing tips and discard or use them for making stock. Skin the second joint sections, removing the two small bones, and reserve the meat for the filling.

2 Grind the reserved meat and mix with the filling ingredients.

3 Holding the large end of the bone on the third section of the wing and using a sharp knife, cut the skin and flesh away from the bone, scraping down and pulling the meat over the small end to form a pocket. Repeat this process with the remaining wing sections.

4 Fill the tiny pockets with the filling. Mix the dried bread-crumbs and the sesame seeds together. Place the breadcrumb mixture and the beaten egg in separate dishes.

5 Brush the meat with beaten egg and roll in breadcrumbs to cover. Chill and repeat to make a second layer, forming a thick coating. Chill until ready to fry.

6 Preheat the oven to 350°F. Heat 2 inches of oil in a heavy pan until hot but not smoking, or the breadcrumbs will burn. Gently fry two or three wings at a time until golden brown, remove and drain on paper towels. Complete the cooking in the preheated oven for 15–20 minutes, until tender.

Penne with Chicken and Ham Sauce

A meal in itself, this colorful pasta sauce is perfect for lunch or dinner.

INGREDIENTS

Serves 4

3 cups penne
2 tablespoons butter
1 onion, chopped
1 garlic clove, chopped
1 bay leaf
2 cups dry white wine
$^2/_3$ cup crème fraîche
1$^1/_2$ cups cooked chicken, skinned, boned and diced
$^2/_3$ cup cooked lean ham, diced
1 cup grated Gouda cheese
1 tablespoon chopped fresh mint
salt and black pepper
finely shredded fresh mint, to garnish

1 Cook the pasta in plenty of water, following the instructions on the package.

2 Heat the butter in a large frying pan and fry the onion for 10 minutes, until softened.

3 Add the garlic, bay leaf and wine and bring to a boil. Boil rapidly until reduced by half. Remove the bay leaf, then stir in the crème fraîche and bring back to a boil.

4 Add the chicken, ham and cheese and simmer for 5 minutes, stirring occasionally, until heated through.

5 Add the mint and seasoning. Drain the pasta and turn it into a large serving bowl. Toss with the sauce immediately and garnish with shredded mint.

COOK'S TIP

Crème fraîche is a richer, full-fat French cream with a slightly acidic taste. If you can't find any, substitute sour cream.

Tagliatelle with Chicken and Herb Sauce

This wine-flavored sauce is best served with green salad.

INGREDIENTS

Serves 4

2 tablespoons olive oil

1 red onion, cut into wedges

12 ounces tagliatelle

1 garlic clove, chopped

2^1/$_2$ cups chicken, diced

1^1/$_4$ cups dry vermouth

3 tablespoons chopped fresh mixed herbs

^{2}/$_3$ cup ricotta or farmer's cheese

salt and black pepper

shredded fresh mint, to garnish

1 Heat the oil in a large frying pan and fry the onion for 10 minutes until softened, and the layers begin to separate.

2 Cook the pasta in plenty of water, following the instructions on the package.

COOK'S TIP

If you don't want to use vermouth, use dry white wine instead. Orvieto and frascati are two Italian wines that are ideal to use in this sauce.

3 Add the garlic and chicken to the frying pan and fry for 10 minutes, stirring occasionally, until the chicken is browned all over and cooked through.

4 Pour in the vermouth, bring to a boil and boil rapidly until reduced by about half.

5 Stir in the herbs, cheese and seasoning and heat through gently, but do not boil.

6 Drain the pasta thoroughly and toss it with the sauce to coat. Serve immediately, garnished with shredded fresh mint.

Risotto

An Italian dish made with short grain arborio rice, which gives a creamy consistency to this easy one-pan recipe.

INGREDIENTS

Serves 4

1 tablespoon oil

1 cup arborio rice

1 onion, chopped

2 cups ground chicken

2¹/2 cups homemade or canned
    chicken stock

1 red bell pepper, seeded and chopped

1 yellow bell pepper, seeded and chopped

³/4 cup frozen green beans

1¹/2 cups Crimini
    mushrooms, sliced

1 tablespoon chopped fresh parsley

salt and black pepper

fresh parsley, to garnish

3 Pour in the stock and bring to a boil.

4 Stir in the peppers and reduce the heat. Cook for 10 minutes.

5 Add the green beans and mushrooms and cook for another 10 minutes.

6 Stir in the fresh parsley and season well to taste. Cook for 10 minutes, or until the liquid has been absorbed. Serve garnished with fresh parsley.

1 Heat the oil in a large frying pan. Add the rice and cook for 2 minutes, until transparent.

2 Add the onion and ground chicken. Cook for 5 minutes, stirring occasionally.

SALADS
& BARBECUES

∼

Chicken Pitas with Red Coleslaw

Pitas are convenient for simple snacks and packed lunches and it's easy to pack them with lots of fresh, healthy ingredients.

INGREDIENTS

Serves 4

1/4 red cabbage

1 small red onion, finely sliced

2 radishes, thinly sliced

1 red apple, peeled, cored and grated

1 tablespoon lemon juice

3 tablespoons ricotta cheese

1 cooked chicken breast without skin, about 6 ounces

4 large or 8 small pitas

salt and black pepper

chopped fresh parsley, to garnish

1 Remove the tough central spine from the cabbage leaves, then finely shred the leaves using a large sharp knife. Place the shredded cabbage in a bowl and stir in the onion, radishes, apple and lemon juice.

2 Stir the ricotta cheese into the shredded cabbage mixture and season well with salt and pepper. Thinly slice the cooked chicken breast and stir into the cabbage mixture until well coated with ricotta.

3 Sprinkle the pitas with a little water, warm them in a hot oven, then split them along one edge using a round-bladed knife. Divide the filling equally among the pitas, then garnish with chopped fresh parsley.

COOK'S TIP

If the filled pitas need to be made more than an hour in advance, line the pita breads with crisp lettuce leaves before adding the filling.

Caribbean Chicken Kebabs

These kebabs have a rich, sunny Caribbean flavor, and the marinade keeps them moist without the need for oil. Serve with a colorful salad and rice.

INGREDIENTS

Serves 4

1^1/4 pounds chicken breasts, boned and skinned

finely grated rind of 1 lime

2 tablespoons lime juice

1 tablespoon rum or sherry

1 tablespoon light brown sugar

1 teaspoon ground cinnamon

2 mangoes, peeled and cubed

rice and salad, to serve

1 Cut the chicken breasts into bite-size chunks and place in a bowl with the grated lime rind and juice, rum or sherry, sugar and cinnamon. Toss well, cover and marinate for 1 hour.

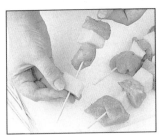

2 Save the juices, and thread the chicken onto four wooden skewers, alternating with the mango cubes.

3 Cook the kebabs under a hot broiler or barbecue for 8–10 minutes, turning occasionally and basting with the reserved juices, until the chicken is tender and golden brown. Serve at once with rice and salad.

COOK'S TIP

The rum or sherry adds a terrific rich flavor, but it is optional so can be omitted if you prefer to make the dish more economical.

Grilled Chicken

The flavor of this dish, known in Indonesia as Ayam Bakur, will be more intense if the chicken is marinated overnight. It is an ideal recipe for a party, because the final broiling, barbecuing or baking can be done at the last minute.

INGREDIENTS

Serves 4

1 chicken, 3–3^{1}/2 pounds
4 garlic cloves, crushed
2 lemon grass stems, lower 2 inches sliced
1 teaspoon ground turmeric
2 cups water
3–4 bay leaves
3 tablespoons each dark and light soy sauce
^{1}/4 cup butter or margarine
salt
boiled rice, to serve

1 Cut the chicken into 4 or 8 portions. Slash the fleshy part of each portion twice and set aside.

2 Grind the garlic, sliced lemon grass, turmeric and salt together into a paste in a food processor or with a mortar and pestle. Rub the paste into the chicken pieces and leave for at least 30 minutes. Wear rubber gloves for this, as the turmeric will stain; or wash your hands immediately after mixing, if you prefer.

3 Transfer the chicken to a wok and pour in the water. Add the bay leaves and bring to a boil. Cover and cook gently for 30 minutes, adding a little more water, if necessary, and stirring occasionally.

4 Just before serving, add the two soy sauces to the pan together with the butter or margarine.

5 Cook until the chicken is well-coated and the sauce has almost been absorbed. Transfer the chicken to a preheated broiler or barbecue, or an oven preheated to 400°F, to complete the cooking. Cook for another 10–15 minutes, turning the pieces often so they become golden brown all over. Take care not to let them burn. Baste with remaining sauce during cooking. Serve with boiled rice.

Dijon Chicken Salad

An attractive dish to serve for lunch with herb and garlic bread.

INGREDIENTS

Serves 4

4 chicken breasts, boned and skinned
mixed salad leaves, such as frisée and
   oakleaf lettuce or radicchio, to serve

For the marinade
2 tablespoons Dijon mustard
3 garlic cloves, crushed
1 tablespoon grated onion
4 tablespoons white wine

For the mustard dressing
2 tablespoons tarragon vinegar
1 teaspoon Dijon mustard
1 teaspoon honey
6 tablespoons olive oil
salt and black pepper

1 Mix all the marinade ingredients in a shallow glass or ceramic dish that is large enough to hold the chicken in a single layer.

2 Turn the chicken over in the marinade to coat completely, cover with plastic wrap and chill in the fridge overnight.

3 Preheat the oven to 375°F. Transfer the chicken and the marinade to an ovenproof dish, cover with foil and bake for about 35 minutes, or until tender. Set aside to cool.

4 Put all the mustard dressing ingredients into a screw-top jar, shake vigorously to emulsify, and adjust the seasoning. (This can be made several days in advance and stored in the fridge.)

5 Slice the chicken thinly, fan out the slices and arrange on a serving dish with the salad leaves.

6 Spoon on some of the mustard dressing and serve.

Lemon Chicken with Guacamole Sauce

The avocado sauce makes an unusual accompaniment to the grilled chicken.

Serves 4

juice of 2 lemons
3 tablespoons olive oil
2 garlic cloves, crushed
4 chicken breast halves, about
    7 ounces each
2 beefsteak tomatoes, cored and halved
salt and black pepper
chopped fresh cilantro, to garnish

For the sauce
1 ripe avocado
$1/4$ cup sour cream
3 tablespoons fresh lemon juice
$1/2$ teaspoon salt
$1/4$ cup water

1 Combine the lemon juice, oil, garlic, $1/2$ teaspoon salt, and a little pepper in a bowl. Stir to mix.

2 Arrange the chicken breasts in one layer, in a shallow glass or ceramic dish. Pour on the lemon mixture and turn to coat evenly. Cover and let stand at least 1 hour at room temperature, or refrigerate overnight.

3 For the sauce, cut the avocado in half, remove the pit, and scrape the flesh into a food processor or blender.

4 Add the sour cream, lemon juice, and salt and process until smooth. Add the water and process just to blend. If necessary, add more water to thin the sauce. Transfer to a bowl, taste and adjust the seasoning, if necessary. Set aside.

5 Preheat the broiler. Also heat a ridged stovetop grill pan. Remove the chicken from the marinade and pat dry.

6 When the grill pan is hot, add the chicken breasts and cook, turning often, until they are cooked through, about 10 minutes.

7 Meanwhile, arrange the tomato halves, cut sides up, on a baking sheet and season lightly with salt and pepper. Broil until hot and bubbling, about 5 minutes.

8 To serve, place a chicken breast, tomato half, and a dollop of avocado sauce on each plate. Sprinkle with cilantro and serve.

VARIATION

To barbecue the chicken, light the barbecue grill, and when the coals are glowing red and covered with gray ash, spread them in a single layer. Set an oiled grill rack about 5 inches above the coals and cook the chicken breasts until lightly charred and cooked through, about 15–20 minutes. Use extra olive oil for basting.

Chicken Liver Kebabs

These may be barbecued outdoors and served with salads and baked potatoes, or broiled indoors and served with rice and broccoli.

INGREDIENTS

Serves 4

4 ounces lean bacon strips

12 ounces chicken livers

12 large pitted prunes

12 cherry tomatoes

8 button mushrooms

2 tablespoons olive oil

1 Cut each strip of bacon into two pieces, wrap a piece around each chicken liver and secure in place with wooden toothpicks.

2 Wrap the pitted prunes around the cherry tomatoes.

3 Thread the bacon-wrapped livers onto metal skewers with the tomatoes, prunes and mushrooms. Brush with oil. Cover the tomatoes and prunes with a strip of foil to protect them while broiling or barbecuing. Cook for 5 minutes on each side.

4 Remove the toothpicks and serve the kebabs immediately.

Citrus Kebabs

Serve on a bed of lettuce leaves and garnish with fresh mint and orange and lemon slices.

INGREDIENTS

Serves 4

4 chicken breasts, skinned and boned
fresh mint sprigs, to garnish
orange, lemon or lime slices, to garnish
  (optional)

For the marinade
finely grated rind and juice of $^1/_2$ orange
finely grated rind and juice of $^1/_2$ small
  lemon or lime
2 tablespoons olive oil
2 tablespoons honey
2 tablespoons chopped fresh mint
$^1/_4$ teaspoon ground cumin
salt and black pepper

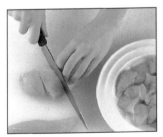

1 Cut the chicken breasts into 1-inch cubes.

2 Mix the marinade ingredients together in a glass or ceramic bowl, add the chicken cubes and marinate for at least 2 hours.

3 Thread the chicken pieces onto skewers and broil or barbecue over low coals for 15 minutes, basting with the marinade and turning frequently. Serve garnished with extra mint and citrus slices, if desired.

Chicken Satay

Marinate the chicken in the satay sauce overnight to allow the flavors to penetrate it. Soak wooden skewers in water overnight to prevent them from burning while cooking.

INGREDIENTS

Serves 4

4 chicken breasts
lemon slices, to garnish
lettuce leaves, to serve
scallions, to serve

For the satay
$^1/_2$ cup crunchy peanut butter
1 small onion, chopped
1 garlic clove, crushed
2 tablespoons chutney
4 tablespoons olive oil
1 teaspoon light soy sauce
2 tablespoons lemon juice
$^1/_4$ teaspoon ground chilies or
  cayenne pepper

1 Put all the satay ingredients into a food processor or blender and process until smooth. Spoon into a large dish.

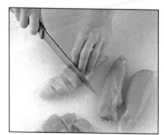

2 Remove all bone and skin from the chicken and cut into 1-inch cubes. Add to the satay mixture and stir to coat the chicken pieces. Cover with plastic wrap and chill for at least 4 hours or, better still, overnight.

3 Preheat the broiler or grill. Thread the chicken pieces onto the wooden skewers.

4 Cook for 10 minutes, brushing occasionally with the satay sauce. Serve on a bed of lettuce and scallions, and garnish with lemon slices.

Chicken and Pasta Salad

This is a delicious way to use up leftover cooked chicken.

INGREDIENTS

Serves 4

2 cups tri-colored pasta twists

2 tablespoons pesto sauce

1 tablespoon olive oil

1 beefsteak tomato

12 pitted black olives

1¹/₂ cups cooked green beans

3 cups cooked chicken, cubed

salt and black pepper

fresh basil, to garnish

1 Cook the pasta in plenty of boiling, salted water until al dente (about 12 minutes or as directed on the package).

2 Drain the pasta and rinse in plenty of cold running water. Put into a bowl and stir in the pesto sauce and olive oil.

3 Peel the tomato, first by placing in boiling water for about 10 seconds and then into cold water, to loosen the skin.

4 Cut the tomato into small cubes and add to the pasta with the olives, seasoning and green beans cut into 1¹/₂-inch lengths. Add the cubed chicken. Toss gently together and transfer to a serving platter. Garnish with fresh basil.

Barbecued Jerk Chicken

Jerk refers to the blend of herb and spice seasoning rubbed into meat before it is roasted over charcoal sprinkled with pimiento berries. In Jamaica, jerk seasoning was originally used only for pork, but jerked chicken is equally good.

INGREDIENTS

Serves 4

8 chicken pieces

For the marinade

1 teaspoon ground allspice

1 teaspoon ground cinnamon

1 teaspoon dried thyme

$1/4$ teaspoon freshly grated nutmeg

2 teaspoons raw sugar

2 garlic cloves, crushed

1 tablespoon finely chopped onion

1 tablespoon chopped scallion

1 tablespoon vinegar

2 tablespoons peanut oil

1 tablespoon lime juice

1 hot chili pepper, chopped

salt and black pepper

lettuce leaves, to serve

1 Combine all the marinade ingredients in a small bowl. Using a fork, mash them together well to form a thick paste.

2 Lay the chicken pieces on a plate or board and make several lengthwise slits in the flesh. Rub the seasoning all over the chicken and into the slits.

3 Place the chicken pieces in a dish, cover with plastic wrap and marinate overnight in the fridge. Shake off any excess seasoning from the chicken. Brush with oil and place either on a baking sheet or a barbecue grill, if barbecuing.

4 Cook under a preheated broiler for 45 minutes, turning often. Or, if barbecuing, light the coals and when ready, cook over the coals for 30 minutes, turning often. Serve hot with lettuce leaves.

COOK'S TIP

The flavor is best if you marinate the chicken overnight.

Grilled Butterflied Rock Cornish Hens

Grilled Rock Cornish hens with an onion and herb dressing.

INGREDIENTS

Serves 4

4 Rock Cornish hens, about 1 pound each,
    butterflied
olive oil
salt and black pepper

For the onion and herb sauce
2 tablespoons dry sherry
2 tablespoons lemon juice
2 tablespoons olive oil
2 ounces scallions, chopped
1 garlic clove, finely chopped
4 tablespoons chopped mixed fresh herbs
    such as tarragon, parsley, thyme,
    marjoram, and lemon balm

1 Preheat the broiler to high, or prepare a charcoal grill.

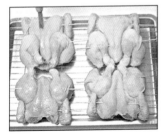

2 Season the butterflied birds, then brush them with a little olive oil. Set them on the rack in the broiler pan about 4 inches from the heat, or on the barbecue grill 6 inches above the coals.

3 Cook for 20–25 minutes, or until tender. Turn and brush with more oil halfway through the cooking time.

4 Meanwhile, to make the sauce, whisk together the sherry, lemon juice, olive oil, scallions and garlic. Season with salt and pepper.

5 When the birds are done, transfer them to a deep serving platter. Whisk the herbs into the sauce, then spoon it on the birds. Cover tightly with another platter or with foil and let rest for 15 minutes before serving.

Chinese-style Chicken Salad

Shredded chicken is served with a tasty peanut sauce.

Serves 4

4 boneless chicken breasts, about
   6 ounces each
4 tablespoons dark soy sauce
pinch of Chinese five-spice powder
a good squeeze of lemon juice
$^1/_2$ cucumber, peeled and cut into
   matchsticks
1 teaspoon salt
3 tablespoons sunflower oil
2 tablespoons sesame oil
1 tablespoon sesame seeds
2 tablespoons dry sherry
2 carrots, cut into matchsticks
8 scallions, shredded
$^1/_2$ cup beansprouts

For the sauce
4 tablespoons crunchy peanut butter
2 teaspoons lemon juice
2 teaspoons sesame oil
$^1/_4$ teaspoon ground hot chilies
1 scallion, finely chopped

1 Put the chicken pieces into a large pan and just cover with water. Add 1 tablespoon of the soy sauce, the Chinese five-spice powder and lemon juice, cover and bring to a boil, then simmer for about 20 minutes.

2 Place the cucumber matchsticks in a colander, sprinkle with the salt and cover with a weighted plate on top. Let drain for 30 minutes.

3 Heat the oils in a large frying pan or wok. Add the sesame seeds, fry for 30 seconds and then stir in the remaining soy sauce and the sherry. Add the carrots and stir-fry for 2–3 minutes. Remove and reserve.

4 Remove the chicken from the pan and let stand until cool enough to handle. Discard the skins and bash the chicken lightly with a rolling pin to loosen the fibers. Slice in strips and reserve.

5 Rinse the cucumber well, pat dry with paper towels and place in a bowl. Add the scallions, beansprouts, cooked carrots, pan juices and shredded chicken, and mix together. Transfer to a shallow dish. Cover and chill for about 1 hour, turning the mixture in the juices once or twice.

6 To make the sauce, cream the peanut butter with the lemon juice, sesame oil and ground chilies, adding a little hot water to form a paste, then stir in the scallion. Arrange the chicken mixture on a serving dish and serve with the peanut sauce.

Fusilli with Chicken, Tomatoes and Broccoli

This is a really hearty main-course salad for a hungry family.

INGREDIENTS

Serves 4

1¹/2 pounds ripe but firm plum tomatoes, quartered
6 tablespoons olive oil
1 teaspoon dried oregano
salt and black pepper
12 ounces broccoli florets
1 small onion, sliced
1 teaspoon dried thyme
1 pound chicken breasts, boned, skinned and cubed
3 garlic cloves, crushed
1 tablespoon fresh lemon juice
1 pound fusilli

1 Preheat the oven to 400°F.

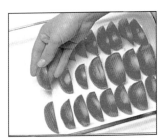

2 Place the tomatoes in a baking dish. Add 1 tablespoon of the oil, the oregano, and ¹/2 teaspoon salt and stir to blend.

3 Bake until the tomatoes are just browned, about 30–40 minutes; do not stir.

4 Meanwhile, bring a large pan of salted water to a boil. Add the broccoli and cook until just tender, about 5 minutes. Drain and set aside. (Alternatively, steam the broccoli until tender.)

5 Heat 2 tablespoons of the oil in a large nonstick frying pan. Add the onion, thyme, chicken cubes and ¹/2 teaspoon salt. Cook over high heat, stirring until the meat is cooked and beginning to brown, 5–7 minutes. Add the garlic and cook 1 minute more, stirring.

6 Remove from the heat. Stir in the lemon juice and season with pepper. Keep warm until the pasta is cooked.

7 Bring another large pan of salted water to a boil. Add the fusilli and cook until just tender (check the instructions on the package for timing). Drain and place in a large bowl. Toss with the remaining oil.

8 Add the broccoli to the chicken mixture. Add to the fusilli. Add the tomatoes and stir gently to blend. Serve immediately.

Swiss Cheese, Chicken and Tongue Salad

The rich sweet flavors of this salad marry well with the peppery watercress. A minted lemon dressing freshens the overall effect. Serve with new potatoes.

INGREDIENTS

Serves 4

2 free-range chicken breasts, skinned and boned

$^1/_2$ chicken bouillon cube

8 ounces sliced beef tongue or ham, $^1/_4$ inch thick

8 ounces Gruyère cheese

1 red leaf lettuce

1 Boston or curly endive lettuce

1 bunch watercress

2 green apples, cored and sliced

3 stalks celery, sliced

4 tablespoons sesame seeds, toasted

salt, black pepper and nutmeg

Dressing

5 tablespoons peanut or sunflower oil

1 teaspoon sesame oil

3 tablespoons lemon juice

2 teaspoons chopped fresh mint

3 drops Tabasco sauce

1 Place the chicken breasts in a shallow saucepan, cover with 1$^1/_4$ cups water, add the $^1/_2$ bouillon cube and bring to a boil. Put the lid on the pan and simmer for 15 minutes. Drain, reserving the stock for another occasion, then cool the chicken under cold running water.

2 To make the dressing, measure the two oils, lemon juice, mint and Tabasco sauce into a screw-top jar and shake. Cut the chicken, tongue and Gruyère cheese into fine strips. Moisten with a little dressing and set aside.

3 Combine the salad leaves with the apple and celery, and dress. Distribute among 4 large plates. Pile the chicken, tongue and cheese in the center, sprinkle with toasted sesame seeds, season with salt, pepper and freshly grated nutmeg and serve.

Chicken Liver, Bacon and Tomato Salad

Warm salads are especially welcome during the autumn months when the evenings are growing shorter and cooler. Try this rich salad with sweet spinach and bitter leaves of frisée lettuce.

INGREDIENTS

Serves 4

8 ounces young spinach, stems removed

1 frisée lettuce or curly endive

7 tablespoons peanut or sunflower oil

6 ounces rindless unsmoked bacon, cut into strips

3 ounces day-old bread, crusts removed and cut into short fingers

1 pound chicken livers

4 ounces cherry tomatoes

salt and black pepper

1 Place the salad leaves in a salad bowl. Heat 4 tablespoons of the oil in a large frying pan. Add the bacon and cook for 3–4 minutes, or until crisp and brown. Remove the bacon with a slotted spoon and drain on paper towels.

2 To make the croutons, fry the bread in the bacon-flavored oil, tossing until crisp and golden. Drain on paper towels.

3 Heat the remaining 3 tablespoons oil in the frying pan, add the chicken livers and fry briskly for 2–3 minutes. Pour over the salad leaves, and add the bacon, croutons and tomatoes. Season, toss and serve.

Wild Rice and Chicken Salad

Once you have cooked the wild rice, this is a very simple salad to make.

INGREDIENTS

Serves 4

1 cup (dry-weight) wild rice, boiled or
    steamed
2 stalks celery, thinly sliced
2 ounces scallions, chopped
$1^{1}/_{2}$ cups small button mushrooms,
    quartered
1 pound cooked chicken breast, diced
$^{1}/_{2}$ cup vinaigrette dressing
1 teaspoon fresh thyme leaves
2 pears, peeled, halved and cored
$^{1}/_{4}$ cup walnut pieces, toasted

1 Combine cooled cooked wild rice with the celery, scallions, mushrooms and chicken in a bowl.

2 Add the dressing and thyme; toss well together.

3 Thinly slice the pear halves lengthwise without cutting through the stem end and spread the slices into a fan. Divide the salad among 4 plates. Garnish each with a fanned pear half and walnuts.

COOKING WILD RICE

To boil: Add the rice to a large pot of boiling salted water (about four parts water to each one of rice). Bring back to a gentle boil and cook for 45–50 minutes, or until the rice is tender but still firm and has begun to split open. Drain well.
To steam: Put the rice in a saucepan with the measured quantity of salted water. Bring to a boil, cover and steam over very low heat for 45–50 minutes, or until tender. Cook uncovered for the last 5 minutes to evaporate excess water.

Warm Chicken Liver Salad

Although warm salads may seem fussy or trendy, there are times when they are just right. Serve this delicious combination as either a first course or a light meal, with bread to dip into the dressing.

INGREDIENTS

Serves 4

4 ounces each fresh young spinach, arugula and red leaf lettuce

2 pink grapefruit

6 tablespoons sunflower oil

2 teaspoons sesame oil

2 teaspoons soy sauce

8 ounces chicken livers, chopped

salt and black pepper

1 Wash, dry and tear up all the leaves. Mix them well in a large salad bowl.

2 Carefully cut away all the peel and white pith from the grapefruit, then segment them, saving the juice. Add the grapefruit to the salad leaves.

3 To make the dressing, combine 4 tablespoons of the sunflower oil with the sesame oil, soy sauce, seasoning and grapefruit juice to taste.

4 Heat the rest of the sunflower oil in a small pan and cook the livers, stirring gently, until firm and lightly browned.

5 Pour the chicken livers and dressing over the salad and serve at once.

COOK'S TIP

Chicken or turkey livers are ideal for this recipe, and there's no need to leave them to defrost completely before cooking.

Orange Chicken Salad

A refreshing and very delicately flavored rice salad.

Serves 4

3 large seedless oranges

1 cup long-grain rice

2 cups water

³/4 cup vinaigrette dressing, made with
red wine vinegar and a mixture of olive
and vegetable oils

2 teaspoons Dijon mustard

¹/2 teaspoon sugar

1 pound cooked chicken, diced

3 tablespoons chopped chives

¹/2 cup roasted cashews

salt and black pepper

cucumber slices, to garnish

1 Thinly peel 1 orange, taking only the colored part of the rind and leaving the white pith.

2 Combine the orange rind, rice and water in a saucepan. Add a pinch of salt. Bring to a boil, then cover and simmer over very low heat for 15–18 minutes, or until the rice is tender and all the water has been absorbed.

3 Peel the remaining oranges and cut out the segments, reserving the juice. Add the orange juice to the vinaigrette dressing. Add the mustard and sugar and whisk to combine well. Taste and add more salt and pepper if needed.

4 When the rice is cooked, remove it from the heat and cool slightly, uncovered. Discard the orange rind.

5 Turn the rice into a bowl and add half of the dressing. Toss well and cool completely.

6 Add the chicken, chives, cashews and orange segments to the rice with the remaining dressing. Toss gently. Serve at room temperature, garnished with cucumber.

Making Vinaigrette Dressing

A good vinaigrette can do more than dress a salad. It can also be used to baste meat, poultry, seafood or vegetables during cooking and it can be used as a flavoring and tenderizing marinade. The basic mixture of oil, vinegar and seasoning lends itself to many variations.

Vinaigrette dressing will keep in the fridge, in a tightly sealed container, for several weeks. Add flavorings, particularly fresh herbs, just before using.

Makes just over ³/4 cup

3 tablespoons wine vinegar

salt and pepper

²/3 cup vegetable or olive oil

1 Put the vinegar, salt and pepper in a bowl and whisk to dissolve the salt. Gradually add the oil, stirring with the whisk. Taste and adjust seasoning.

Grilled Chicken Salad with Lavender

Lavender may seem like an odd salad ingredient, but its delightful scent has a natural affinity with sweet garlic, orange and other wild herbs. A serving of polenta makes this salad both filling and delicious.

INGREDIENTS

Serves 4

4 chicken breasts, boned

3³/4 cups homemade or canned
  chicken stock

1 cup fine polenta

4 tablespoons butter

1 pound young spinach

6 ounces lamb's lettuce or other very
  young lettuce

8 sprigs fresh lavender

8 small tomatoes, halved

salt and black pepper

Lavender Marinade

6 fresh lavender flowers

2 teaspoons finely grated orange rind

2 cloves garlic, crushed

2 teaspoons honey

salt

2 tablespoons olive oil

2 teaspoons chopped fresh thyme

2 teaspoons chopped fresh marjoram

1 To make the marinade, strip the lavender flowers from the stems and combine with the orange rind, garlic, honey and salt. Add the olive oil and herbs. Slash the chicken deeply, spread the mixture over the chicken and marinate in a cool place for at least 20 minutes.

2 To cook the polenta, bring the chicken stock to a boil in a heavy saucepan. Add the polenta in a steady stream, stirring all the time until thick: this will take 2–3 minutes. Turn the cooked polenta out onto a 1-inch-deep buttered tray and allow to cool.

3 Heat the broiler to medium. (If using a barbecue, let the embers settle to a steady glow.) Grill the chicken for about 15 minutes, turning once.

4 Cut the polenta into 1-inch cubes with a wet knife. Heat the butter in a large frying pan and fry the polenta until golden.

5 Wash the salad leaves and spin dry, then divide among 4 large plates. Slice each chicken breast and lay over the salad. Place the polenta among the salad, garnish with sprigs of lavender and tomatoes, season and serve.

Maryland Salad

Barbecued chicken, corn, bacon, banana and watercress combine here in a sensational main course salad. Serve with baked potatoes and a pat of butter.

Serves 4

4 chicken breasts, boned

8 ounces rindless unsmoked bacon

4 ears corn

3 tablespoons butter, softened

4 ripe bananas, peeled and halved

4 firm tomatoes, halved

1 greenleaf or Boston lettuce

1 bunch watercress

salt and black pepper

For the dressing

5 tablespoons peanut oil

1 tablespoon white wine vinegar

2 teaspoons maple syrup

2 teaspoons mild mustard

1 Season the chicken breasts, brush with oil and barbecue or broil for 15 minutes, turning once. Broil the bacon for 8–10 minutes, or until crisp.

2 Bring a large saucepan of salted water to a boil. Shuck and trim the corn. Boil for 3–5 minutes. For extra flavor, brush with butter and brown over the barbecue or under the broiler. Barbecue or broil the bananas and tomatoes for 6–8 minutes, brushing these with butter too, if you wish.

3 To make the dressing, combine the oil, vinegar, maple syrup and mustard with seasoning and 1 tablespoon water in a screw-top jar and shake well.

4 Wash, spin thoroughly and dress the salad leaves.

5 Distribute the salad leaves among 4 large plates. Slice the chicken and arrange over the leaves with the bacon, banana, corn and tomatoes.

Grilled Chicken with Pica de Gallo Salsa

This dish originated in Mexico. Its hot fruity flavors form the essence of Tex-Mex cooking.

INGREDIENTS

Serves 4

4 chicken breasts

pinch of celery salt and cayenne pepper
  combined

2 tablespoons vegetable oil

corn chips, to serve

For the salsa

10 ounces watermelon

6 ounces cantaloupe

1 small red onion

1–2 green chilies

2 tablespoons lime juice

4 tablespoons chopped fresh cilantro

pinch of salt

1 Heat the broiler or barbecue to medium. Slash the chicken breasts deeply to speed up the cooking.

2 Season the chicken with the celery salt and cayenne, brush with oil and broil or barbecue for about 15 minutes.

3 To make the salsa, remove the rind and as many seeds as you can from the melons. Finely dice the flesh and put it into a bowl.

4 Finely chop the onion, split the chilies (discarding the seeds, which contain most of the heat) and chop. Take care when handling cut chilies. Mix with the melon.

5 Add the lime juice and cilantro, and season with salt. Put the salsa into a small bowl.

6 Arrange the grilled chicken on a plate and serve with the salsa and a handful of corn chips.

COOK'S TIP

To capture the spirit of Tex-Mex food, cook the chicken over a grill and eat shaded from the hot summer sun.

Coronation Chicken

A summer favorite – serve with a crisp green salad.

INGREDIENTS

Serves 8

$^1/_2$ lemon

1 chicken, 5–5$^1/_4$ pounds

1 onion, quartered

1 carrot, quartered

large bouquet garni

8 black peppercorns, crushed

salt

watercress sprigs, to garnish

For the sauce

1 small onion, chopped

1 tablespoon butter

1 tablespoon curry paste

1 tablespoon tomato paste

$^1/_2$ cup red wine

1 bay leaf

juice of $^1/_2$ lemon, or more to taste

2–3 teaspoons apricot jam

1$^1/_4$ cups good-quality
    mayonnaise

$^1/_2$ cup whipping cream, whipped

salt and black pepper

1 Put the lemon half in the chicken cavity, then place the chicken in a saucepan that it just fits. Add the vegetables, bouquet garni, peppercorns and salt.

2 Add enough water to cover two-thirds of the chicken, bring to a boil, then cover and cook gently for 1$^1/_2$ hours, or until the juices run clear.

3 Transfer to a large bowl, pour the cooking liquid over it and let it cool. Skin and bone the chicken, then chop the flesh.

4 To make the sauce, cook the onion in the butter until soft. Add the curry paste, tomato paste, wine, bay leaf and lemon juice, then cook for 10 minutes. Add the apricot jam; sieve and cool.

5 Beat the sauce into the mayonnaise. Fold in the cream; add seasoning, then stir in the chicken and garnish with watercress.

Peanut Chicken in Pineapple Boats

An impressive-looking dish to serve at a dinner party.

INGREDIENTS

Serves 4

2 small ripe pineapples
1 1/2 cups cooked chicken breast, cut into
    bite-size pieces
2 stalks celery, diced
3 scallions, white and green parts,
    chopped
8 ounces seedless green grapes
1 1/2 ounces salted peanuts, coarsely
    chopped

For the dressing

3 ounces smooth peanut butter
1/2 cup mayonnaise
2 tablespoons cream or milk
1 garlic clove, finely chopped
1 teaspoon mild curry powder
1 tablespoon apricot jam
salt and black pepper

1 Make 4 pineapple boats from the pineapples. Cut the fruit removed from the boats into bite-size pieces.

2 Combine the pineapple flesh, chicken, celery, scallions and grapes in a bowl.

3 Put all the dressing ingredients in another bowl and mix with a wooden spoon or whisk until evenly blended. Season with salt and pepper. (The dressing will be thick, but will be thinned by the juices from the pineapple.)

4 Add the dressing to the pineapple and chicken mixture. Fold together gently but thoroughly.

5 Divide the chicken salad among the pineapple boats. Sprinkle the peanuts over the top before serving.

Warm Chicken and Cilantro Salad

This salad needs to be served warm to make the most of the wonderful sesame and cilantro flavoring. It makes a simple first course or a delicious light lunch dish.

INGREDIENTS

Serves 6

4 medium chicken breasts, boned and
    skinned
8 ounces snow peas
2 heads decorative lettuce such as red leaf
    or oakleaf
3 carrots, peeled and cut into small
    matchsticks
$2^3/4$ cups button mushrooms, sliced
6 strips bacon, fried, drained on paper
    towels and crumbled
1 tablespoon chopped fresh cilantro
    leaves, to garnish

Dressing
$^1/2$ cup lemon juice
2 tablespoons wholegrain mustard
1 cup olive oil
4 tablespoons sesame oil
1 teaspoon coriander seeds, crushed

1 Mix all the dressing ingredients in a bowl. Place the chicken breasts in a shallow dish and pour on half the dressing. Chill overnight, and store the remaining dressing in the fridge.

2 Cook the snow peas for 2 minutes in boiling water, then cool under cold running water to stop them from cooking any longer. Tear the lettuces into small pieces and mix the other salad ingredients and the bacon together. Arrange all these in individual serving dishes.

3 Broil the chicken breasts until cooked through, then slice them on the diagonal into quite thin pieces. Divide among the bowls of salad, and add some dressing to each dish. Combine quickly and sprinkle some fresh cilantro over each bowl.

Sweet and Sour Kebabs

This marinade contains sugar and will burn very easily, so grill the kebabs slowly, turning often. It is delicious served with Harlequin Rice.

INGREDIENTS

Serves 4

2 chicken breasts, boned and
    skinned
8 pickling onions or 2 medium onions
4 strips rindless lean bacon
3 firm bananas
1 red bell pepper, seeded and sliced

For the marinade
2 tablespoons light brown sugar

1 tablespoon Worcestershire sauce
2 tablespoons lemon juice
salt and black pepper

For the Harlequin Rice
2 tablespoons olive oil
generous 1 cup cooked rice
1 cup cooked peas
1 small red bell pepper, seeded
    and diced

1 Mix together the marinade ingredients. Cut each chicken breast into four pieces, add to the marinade, cover and leave for at least 4 hours or preferably overnight in the fridge.

2 Peel the pickling onions, blanch them in boiling water for 5 minutes and drain. If using medium onions, quarter them after blanching.

3 Cut each strip of bacon in half. Peel the bananas and cut each into three pieces. Wrap a strip of bacon around each piece of banana.

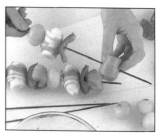

4 Thread onto metal skewers with the chicken pieces, onions and pepper slices. Brush with the marinade.

5 Broil or grill over low coals for 15 minutes, turning and basting frequently with the marinade. Keep warm while you prepare the rice.

6 Heat the oil in a frying pan and add the rice, peas and diced pepper. Stir until heated through and serve with the kebabs.

Chicken and Fruit Salad

The chickens may be cooked a day before eating, and the salad can be quickly put together for lunch.

INGREDIENTS

Serves 8

4 sprigs tarragon or rosemary

2 chickens, 4 pounds each

5 tablespoons softened butter

²/₃ cup homemade or canned
   chicken stock

²/₃ cup white wine

1 cup walnut pieces

1 small cantaloupe

lettuce leaves

1 pound seedless grapes or pitted cherries

salt and black pepper

For the dressing

2 tablespoons tarragon vinegar

¹/₂ cup light olive oil

2 tablespoons chopped mixed fresh herbs,
   such as parsley, mint and tarragon

1 Preheat the oven to 400°F. Put the herb sprigs inside the chickens and season. Tie the chickens with string. Spread the chickens with 4 tablespoons of the softened butter, place in a roasting pan and pour in the stock. Cover loosely with foil and roast for about 1¹/₂ hours, basting twice, until the skin is browned and the juices run clear. Remove the chickens from the roasting pan.

2 Add the wine to the roasting pan. Bring to a boil and cook until syrupy. Strain and let cool. Heat the remaining butter in a frying pan and gently fry the walnuts until browned. Drain and cool. Scoop the melon into balls or cut into cubes; cut up the chickens.

3 To make the dressing, whisk the vinegar and oil together with a little salt and freshly ground black pepper. Remove all the fat from the chicken juices and add these to the dressing with the herbs. Adjust the seasoning.

4 Arrange the chicken pieces on a bed of lettuce, sprinkle with the grapes and melon balls and spoon on the herb dressing. Sprinkle with toasted walnuts.

Warm Stir-fried Salad

Warm salads are becoming increasingly popular because they are delicious and nutritious. Arrange the salad leaves on four individual plates, so the hot stir-fry can be served straight from the wok, making sure the lettuce remains crisp and the chicken warm.

INGREDIENTS

Serves 4

2 chicken breasts, about 8 ounces each, boned and skinned
1 tablespoon chopped fresh tarragon
2-inch piece fresh ginger, peeled and finely chopped
3 tablespoons light soy sauce
1 tablespoon sugar
1 tablespoon sunflower oil
1 head Chinese lettuce
$^1/_2$ frisée lettuce or curly endive, torn into bite-size pieces
1 cup unsalted cashews
2 large carrots, peeled and cut into fine strips
salt and black pepper

1 Cut the chicken into fine strips and place in a bowl.

2 To make the marinade, mix together in a bowl the tarragon, ginger, soy sauce, sugar and seasoning.

3 Pour the marinade over the chicken strips and marinate for 2–4 hours.

4 Strain the chicken from the marinade, reserving the liquid. Heat a wok or large frying pan, then add the oil. When the oil is hot, stir-fry the chicken for 3 minutes, add the marinade and simmer for 2–3 minutes.

5 Slice the Chinese lettuce and arrange on a plate with the frisée. Toss the cashews and carrots together with the chicken and sauce, pile on top of the bed of lettuce and serve immediately.

Indonesian-style Satay Chicken

Use boneless chicken thighs to give a good flavor to these satays.

INGREDIENTS

Serves 4

^{1}/2 cup raw peanuts

3 tablespoons vegetable oil

1 small onion, finely chopped

1-inch piece fresh ginger, peeled and
finely chopped

1 clove garlic, crushed

1^1/2 pounds chicken thighs, skinned and
cut into cubes

3^1/2 ounces creamed coconut, coarsely
chopped

1 tablespoon chili sauce

^{1}/4 cup crunchy peanut butter

1 teaspoon dark brown sugar

^{2}/3 cup milk

^{1}/4 teaspoon salt

1 Shell and rub the skins from the peanuts, then soak them in a bowl with enough water to cover, for 1 minute. Drain the peanuts and carefully cut them into fine slivers.

2 Heat a wok or large frying pan and add 1 teaspoon of the oil. When the oil is hot, stir-fry the peanuts for 1 minute, or until crisp and golden. Remove them with a slotted spoon and drain on paper towels.

3 Add the remaining oil to the hot wok. When the oil is hot, add the onion, ginger and garlic and stir-fry for 2–3 minutes, or until softened but not browned. Remove and drain on paper towels.

4 Add the chicken and stir-fry for 3–4 minutes, or until crisp on all sides.

5 Thread onto pre-soaked bamboo skewers and keep warm in a low oven.

6 Add the creamed coconut to the hot wok in small pieces and stir-fry until melted. Add the chili sauce, peanut butter and cooked onion, ginger and garlic, and simmer for 2 minutes. Stir in the sugar, milk and salt and simmer for another 3 minutes. Serve the skewered chicken hot, with a dash of the hot dipping sauce sprinkled with the peanuts.

PASTRIES
& PIES

~

Curried Chicken and Apricot Pie

This sweet and sour pie is unusually enticing. Use boneless turkey instead of chicken, if you wish.

Serves 6

2 tablespoons sunflower oil

1 large onion, chopped

1 pound chicken, boned and roughly
    chopped

1 tablespoon curry paste or powder

2 tablespoons apricot or peach chutney

$^{1}/_{2}$ cup dried apricots, halved

4 ounces cooked carrots, sliced

1 teaspoon mixed dried herbs

4 tablespoons crème fraîche or sour cream

12 ounces ready-made shortcrust pastry

a little egg or milk, to glaze

salt and black pepper

3 Roll out the pastry to 1 inch wider than the pie dish. Cut a strip of pastry from the edge. Damp the rim of the dish, press on the strip, then brush with water and place the sheet of pastry on top, pressing to seal.

4 Preheat the oven to 375°F. Trim any excess pastry and use it to make an attractive pattern on the top, if you wish. Brush all over with beaten egg or milk and bake for 40 minutes, until crisp and golden.

1 Heat the oil in a large pan and fry the onion and chicken until lightly browned. Add the curry paste or powder and fry for another 2 minutes.

2 Add the chutney, apricots, carrots, herbs and crème fraîche to the pan with seasoning. Mix well and then transfer to a deep 5-cup pie dish.

Chicken Pastries with Herb Butter

A herb-coated, buttery chicken fillet wrapped up in crisp pastry.

INGREDIENTS

Serves 4

4 chicken breast fillets, skinned

3/4 cup butter, softened

6 tablespoons chopped mixed fresh herbs, such as thyme, parsley, oregano and rosemary

1 teaspoon lemon juice

5 large sheets filo pastry, defrosted if frozen

1 egg, beaten

2 tablespoons grated Parmesan cheese

salt and black pepper

1 Season the chicken fillets and fry in 2 tablespoons of the butter until lightly browned. Allow to cool.

2 Preheat the oven to 375°F. Put the remaining butter, the herbs, lemon juice and seasoning in a food processor and process until smooth. Melt half the herb butter.

3 Take one sheet of filo pastry and brush with herb butter. Cover the rest of the pastry with a damp dish towel. Fold the pastry sheet in half and brush again with butter. Place a chicken fillet about 1 inch from the top end.

4 Dot the chicken with a quarter of the remaining herb butter. Fold in the sides of the pastry, then roll up to enclose it completely. Place seam-side down on a lightly greased baking sheet. Repeat with the other chicken fillets.

5 Brush the filo pastries with beaten egg. Cut the last sheet of filo into strips, then crumple and arrange on top. Brush them once again with the egg glaze, then sprinkle with Parmesan cheese. Bake for about 35–40 minutes, until golden brown. Serve hot.

Kotopita

This is based on a Greek chicken pie. Serve hot or cold with a typical Greek salad made from tomatoes, cucumber, onions and feta cheese.

Serves 4

10 ounces filo pastry

2 tablespoons olive oil

$^1/_2$ cup chopped toasted
   almonds

2 tablespoons milk

For the filling

1 tablespoon olive oil

1 medium onion, finely chopped

1 garlic clove, crushed

1 pound cooked chicken, boned

$^1/_4$ cup crumbled feta cheese

2 eggs, beaten

1 tablespoon chopped fresh
   flat-leaf parsley

1 tablespoon chopped fresh cilantro

1 tablespoon chopped fresh mint

salt and black pepper

1 To make the filling, heat the oil in a large frying pan and cook the chopped onion gently until tender. Add the crushed garlic and cook for another 2 minutes. Transfer to a bowl.

2 Remove the skin from the chicken and grind or chop finely. Add to the onion with the rest of the filling ingredients. Mix thoroughly and season with salt and freshly ground black pepper.

3 Preheat the oven to 375°F. Have a damp dish towel ready to keep the filo pastry covered at all times. You will need to work fast, as the pastry dries out very quickly when exposed to air. Unroll the pastry and cut the whole batch into a 12-inch square.

4 Taking half the sheets (cover the remainder), brush one sheet with a little olive oil, lay it on a well-greased 5-cup oven-proof dish.

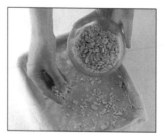

5 Sprinkle with a few chopped almonds. Repeat with the other pastry sheets, overlapping them alternately into the dish. Spoon in the filling and cover in the same way with the remaining pastry.

6 Fold in the edges and mark a diamond pattern on the surface with a sharp knife. Brush with milk and sprinkle on the rest of the almonds. Bake for 20–30 minutes, or until golden brown.

Old-fashioned Chicken Pie

The chicken can be roasted and the sauce prepared a day in advance. Allow to cool completely before covering with pastry and baking. Make into four individual pies if you prefer but bake for 10 minutes less.

Serves 4

3–3¹/₂ pounds chicken

1 onion, quartered

1 sprig fresh tarragon or rosemary

2 tablespoons butter

1¹/₂ cups button mushrooms

2 tablespoons all-purpose flour

1¹/₄ cups homemade or canned
   chicken stock

4 ounces cooked ham, diced

2 tablespoons chopped fresh parsley

1 pound frozen puff pastry or pie pastry,
   defrosted

1 egg, beaten

salt and black pepper

1 Preheat the oven to 400°F. Put the chicken into a casserole, along with the quartered onion and the herbs. Add 1¹/₄ cups water and season. Cover and roast for about 1¹/₄ hours, or until the chicken is tender.

2 Remove the chicken and strain the liquid into a measuring cup. Cool. Remove any fat that settles on the surface. Add enough water to make 1¹/₄ cups and reserve for the sauce.

3 Remove the chicken from the bones and cut into large cubes. Melt the butter in a pan, add the mushrooms and cook for 2–3 minutes. Sprinkle in the flour and gradually blend in the stock.

4 Bring to a boil, season to taste and add the ham, chicken and parsley. Turn into a large pie pan and let cool.

5 Roll out the pastry on a lightly floured surface to 2 inches larger than the pie pan. Cut a narrow strip of pastry to place around the edge of the dish. Dampen with a little water and stick to the rim of the dish. Brush the strip with beaten egg.

6 Lay the pastry loosely over the pie, taking care not to stretch it. Press firmly onto the rim. Using a sharp knife, trim away the excess pastry and knock up the sides to encourage the pastry to rise. Crimp the edge neatly and cut a hole in the center of the pie. This allows steam to escape during cooking. Decorate with pastry leaves and chill until ready to bake.

7 Brush the pastry with beaten egg (taking care not to glaze over the sides of the pastry). Bake in the oven for 35–45 minutes, until well risen and nicely browned all over.

Chicken and Mushroom Pie

Use a mixture of dried and fresh mushrooms for this pie.

INGREDIENTS

Serves 6

$1/4$ cup dried porcini mushrooms
4 tablespoons butter
2 tablespoons all-purpose flour
1 cup chicken stock, warmed
$1/4$ cup whipping cream or milk
1 onion, coarsely chopped
2 carrots, sliced
2 stalks celery, coarsely chopped
$3/4$ cup fresh mushrooms, quartered
3 cups cooked chicken meat, cubed
$1/2$ cup fresh or frozen peas
salt and black pepper
beaten egg, for glazing

For the crust

2 cups all-purpose flour
$1/4$ teaspoon salt
$1/2$ cup cold butter, cut into pieces
$1/3$ cup crisco or vegetable shortening
4–8 tablespoons icewater

1 To make the crust, sift the flour and salt into a bowl. Cut in the butter and shortening until the mixture resembles breadcrumbs. Sprinkle with 6 tablespoons icewater and mix until the dough holds together. Add a little more water, 1 tablespoon at a time if necessary.

2 Gather the dough into a ball and flatten into a disk. Wrap in waxed paper and chill at least 30 minutes.

3 Place the porcini mushrooms in a small bowl. Add hot water to cover and soak until soft, about 30 minutes. Lift out of the water with a slotted spoon, to leave any grit behind, and drain. Discard the soaking water.

4 Preheat the oven to 375°F.

5 Melt 2 tablespoons of the butter in a heavy saucepan. Whisk in the flour and cook until bubbling, whisking constantly. Add the warm stock and cook over medium heat, whisking, until the mixture boils. Cook 2–3 minutes more. Whisk in the cream or milk. Season with salt and pepper. Put to one side.

6 Heat the remaining butter in a large nonstick frying pan until foamy. Add the onion and carrots and cook until softened, about 5 minutes. Add the celery and fresh mushrooms and cook 5 minutes more. Stir in the chicken, peas, and drained porcini mushrooms.

7 Add the chicken mixture to the sauce and stir. Taste for seasoning. Transfer to a rectangular 10-cup baking dish.

8 Roll out the dough to about $1/8$ inch thick. Cut out a rectangle about 1 inch larger all around than the dish. Lay the rectangle of dough over the filling. Make a decorative crimped edge by pushing the index finger of one hand between the thumb and index finger of the other.

9 Cut several vents in the top crust to allow steam to escape. Brush with the egg to glaze.

10 Press together the dough trimmings, then roll out again. Cut into strips and lay them over the top crust. Glaze again. If desired, roll small balls of dough and set them in the "windows" in the lattice.

11 Bake until the top crust is browned, about 30 minutes. Serve the pie hot.

Chicken en Croûte

Chicken breasts, layered with herbs and orange-flavored stuffing and wrapped in light puff pastry, make an impressive dish to serve at a dinner party.

INGREDIENTS

Serves 8

1 pound frozen puff pastry, defrosted
4 large chicken breasts, boned and skinned
1 egg, beaten

For the stuffing

1 cup thinly sliced leeks
1/3 cup chopped lean bacon
2 tablespoons butter
2 cups fresh white breadcrumbs
2 tablespoons chopped fresh herbs, such
  as parsley, thyme, marjoram and chives
grated rind of 1 large orange
1 egg, beaten
salt and black pepper

1 To make the stuffing, cook the sliced leeks and bacon in the butter until soft. Put the breadcrumbs into a bowl with the mixed herbs and plenty of seasoning. Add the leeks, bacon, butter and the grated orange rind and bind together with the beaten egg. If the mixture is too dry and crumbly, you can stir in a little orange juice or chicken stock to bring it to a moist consistency.

2 Roll out the pastry to a large rectangle 12 x 16 inches. Trim the edges and reserve for decorating the top.

3 Place the chicken breasts between two pieces of plastic wrap and flatten to a thickness of 1/4 inch with a rolling pin. Spread a third of the leek stuffing over the center of the pastry. Lay two chicken breasts side-by-side on top of the stuffing. Cover the chicken breasts with another third of the stuffing, then repeat with the remaining chicken breasts and the rest of the stuffing.

4 Make a cut diagonally from each corner of the pastry to the chicken. Brush the pastry with beaten egg.

5 Bring up the sides and overlap them slightly. Trim away any excess pastry before folding the ends over like a package. Turn over onto a greased baking tray, so that the seams are underneath. Shape neatly and trim any excess pastry.

6 With a sharp knife, lightly criss-cross the pastry into a diamond pattern. Brush with beaten egg, and cut leaves from the trimmings to decorate the top. Bake at 400°F for 50–60 minutes, or until well risen and golden brown on top.

Chicken Pastitsio

A traditional Greek pastitsio is a rich, high-fat dish made with ground beef, but this lighter version with chicken is just as tasty.

INGREDIENTS

Serves 4–6

1 pound lean ground chicken

1 large onion, finely chopped

4 tablespoons tomato paste

1 cup red wine or stock

1 teaspoon ground cinnamon

2^1/$_2$ cups macaroni

1^1/$_4$ cups milk

2 tablespoons margarine

4 tablespoons all-purpose flour

1 teaspoon grated nutmeg

2 tomatoes, sliced

4 tablespoons whole-wheat breadcrumbs

salt and black pepper

green salad, to serve

1 Preheat the oven to 425°F. Fry the ground chicken and chopped onion in a nonstick pan without fat, stirring occasionally until lightly browned.

2 Stir in the tomato paste, red wine and cinnamon. Season, then cover and simmer for 5 minutes, stirring occasionally. Remove from the heat.

3 Cook the macaroni in plenty of boiling, salted water until just tender, then drain.

4 Layer the macaroni with the chicken mixture in a wide ovenproof dish.

5 Place the milk, margarine and flour in a saucepan and whisk over medium heat until thickened and smooth. Add the nutmeg and season to taste.

6 Pour the sauce evenly over the pasta and meat layers. Arrange the tomato slices on top and sprinkle whole-wheat breadcrumbs over the surface.

7 Bake for 30–35 minutes, or until golden brown and bubbling. Serve hot with a fresh green salad.

Chicken and Game Pie

A rich filling of chicken and dark meat, spiced with ginger.

Serves 4

1 pound boneless chicken and game meat
(plus the carcasses and bones)
1 small onion, halved
2 bay leaves
2 carrots, halved
a few black peppercorns
1 tablespoon oil
3 ounces lean bacon, rinded and
chopped
1 tablespoon all-purpose flour
3 tablespoons sweet sherry or Madeira
2 teaspoons ground ginger
grated rind and juice of $^1/_2$ orange
12 ounces frozen puff pastry, defrosted
beaten egg or milk, to glaze
salt and black pepper

1 Place the carcasses and bones in a pan, with any giblets and half the onion, the bay leaves, carrots and black peppercorns. Cover with water and bring to a boil. Simmer until reduced to about $1^1/_4$ cups, then strain the stock.

2 Cut the chicken and game meat into even-size pieces. Chop the remaining onion, then fry in the oil until softened. Then add the bacon and meat and fry for a few minutes. Sprinkle on the flour and stir until beginning to brown. Gradually add the stock, stirring as it thickens, then add the sherry or Madeira, ginger, orange rind and juice, and seasoning. Simmer for 20 minutes.

3 Transfer to a 4-cup pie pan and allow to cool slightly. Use a pie funnel to help hold up the pastry.

4 Preheat the oven to 425°F. Roll out the pastry to 1 inch larger than the dish. Cut off a $^1/_2$-inch strip all around. Dampen the rim of the pan and press on the strip of pastry. Dampen again and then lift the pastry carefully over the pie, sealing the edges well at the rim. Trim off the excess pastry, use to decorate the top, then brush the pie with egg or milk.

5 Bake the pie for 15 minutes, then reduce the oven temperature to 375°F and bake for another 25–30 minutes.

Chicken and Stilton Pies

These individual pies are wrapped in crisp pie crust and shaped into pastries. They are great for lunch, served hot or cold.

Makes 4

3 cups self-rising flour

$^1/_2$ teaspoon salt

6 tablespoons crisco or vegetable shortening

6 tablespoons butter

4–5 tablespoons cold water

beaten egg, to glaze

For the filling

1 pound chicken thighs, boned and skinned

$^1/_4$ cup chopped walnuts

1 ounce scallions, sliced

$^1/_2$ cup Stilton, crumbled

1 ounce celery, finely chopped

$^1/_2$ teaspoon dried thyme

salt and black pepper

3 Remove any fat from the chicken thighs and cut into small cubes. Mix with the chopped walnuts, scallions, Stilton, celery, thyme and seasoning and divide the filling equally among the four pastry circles.

4 Brush the edge of the pastry with beaten egg and fold over, pinching and crimping the edges together well. Place on a greased baking sheet and bake in the oven for about 45 minutes, or until golden brown.

1 Preheat the oven to 400°F. Mix the flour and salt in a bowl. Rub in the shortening and butter with your fingers until the mixture resembles fine breadcrumbs. Using a knife to cut and stir, mix in the cold water to form a stiff, pliable dough.

2 Turn out onto a work surface and knead lightly until smooth. Divide into four portions and roll out each piece to a thickness of $^1/_4$ inch. Cut into an 8-inch circle.

Chicken Bouche

A spectacular centerpiece, this light pastry shell contains a delicious chicken and mushroom filling with a hint of fruit. Ideal served with freshly cooked vegetables.

INGREDIENTS

Serves 4

1 pound frozen puff pastry, defrosted

beaten egg, to glaze

For the filling

1 tablespoon oil

3 cups ground chicken

4 tablespoons all-purpose flour

$^2/_3$ cup milk

$^2/_3$ cup homemade or canned
   chicken stock

4 scallions, chopped

$^1/_4$ cup redcurrants or raspberries

1 cup button mushrooms, sliced

1 tablespoon chopped fresh tarragon

salt and black pepper

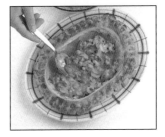

1 Preheat the oven to 400°F. Roll half the pastry out on a lightly floured work surface to a 10-inch oval. Roll out the remainder to an oval of the same size and draw a smaller 8-inch oval in the center.

2 Brush the edge of the first pastry shape with the beaten egg and place the smaller oval on top. Place on a dampened baking sheet and bake for 30 minutes.

3 For the filling, heat the oil in a large pan. Fry the ground chicken for 5 minutes. Add the flour and cook for another minute. Stir in the milk and stock and bring to a boil.

4 Add the scallions, redcurrants and mushrooms. Cook for 20 minutes.

5 Stir in the fresh tarragon and season to taste.

6 Place the pastry bouche on a serving plate, remove the oval center and spoon in the filling. Place the oval lid on top. Serve with freshly cooked vegetables.

VARIATION

You can also use regular pie pastry for this dish and cook as a traditional chicken pie.

HOT & SPICY

~

Simple Curried Chicken

A tasty curry that needs very little preparation.

INGREDIENTS

Serves 4

2 tablespoons vegetable oil
1 onion, chopped
1 green or red bell pepper, seeded
  and diced
1 garlic clove, finely chopped
1^1/$_2$ tablespoons curry powder
^{1}/$_2$ teaspoon dried thyme
1 pound tomatoes, skinned, seeded and
  chopped, or canned chopped tomatoes
2 tablespoons lemon juice
^{1}/$_2$ cup water
2 ounces currants or raisins
salt and black pepper
1 chicken, 3–3^1/$_2$ pounds, skinned and
  cut into 8 pieces
cooked rice, to serve

1 Preheat the oven to 350°F. Heat
the vegetable oil in a wide,
deep frying pan that has a lid and
an ovenproof handle or in a flameproof casserole. Add the chopped
onion, diced bell pepper and
garlic. Cook, stirring occasionally,
until the vegetables are soft.

2 Stir in the curry powder and
thyme, then add the tomatoes,
lemon juice and water. Bring the
sauce to a boil, stirring frequently.
Stir in the currants or raisins.
Season to taste.

3 Put the chicken pieces in the
frying pan or casserole,
arranging them in one layer. Turn
them, so that they are thoroughly
coated with the sauce. Cover the
pan and transfer to the oven. Cook
for about 40 minutes, or until the
chicken is tender. Turn the pieces
halfway through cooking to keep
coated in sauce.

4 Transfer the chicken and sauce
to a warmed serving platter.
Serve with freshly boiled rice.

VARIATION

For Curried Chicken Casserole, a
slightly hotter dish, omit the diced
bell pepper and cook 1^1/$_2$ tablespoons
finely chopped fresh ginger and
1 green chili, seeded and finely
chopped, with the onion and garlic
in a flameproof casserole. In step 2,
stir in the curry powder with
1^3/$_4$ cups plain yogurt; omit the
tomatoes, lemon juice and water.
Add the chicken pieces, cover and
bake at 325°F for 1–1^1/$_4$ hours, or
until the chicken is very tender.

Tangy Chicken

There are few cooking concepts that are better suited to today's busy lifestyle than the all-in-one stir-fry. This delicious example has a Southeast Asian influence.

INGREDIENTS

Serves 4

10 ounces Chinese egg noodles
2 tablespoons vegetable oil
3 scallions, chopped
1 garlic clove, crushed
1-inch piece fresh ginger, peeled
   and grated
1 teaspoon hot paprika
1 teaspoon ground coriander
3 chicken breasts, boned and
   sliced
1 cup sugar-snap peas, trimmed
4 ounces baby corn, halved
8 ounces fresh beansprouts
1 tablespoon cornstarch
3 tablespoons soy sauce
3 tablespoons lemon juice
1 tablespoon sugar
3 tablespoons chopped fresh cilantro
   or scallion tops, to garnish

1 Bring a large saucepan of salted water to a boil. Add the egg noodles and cook according to the instructions on the package. Drain, cover and keep warm.

2 Heat the oil in a wok or large frying pan. Add the scallions and cook over low heat. Mix in the next five ingredients, then stir-fry for 3–4 minutes. Add the next three ingredients and steam briefly. Add the noodles.

3 Combine the cornstarch, soy sauce, lemon juice and sugar in a small bowl. Add to the wok or pan and simmer briefly to thicken. Serve garnished with chopped cilantro or scallion tops.

Chicken with Pineapple

This chicken has a delicate tang and is very tender. The pineapple not only tenderizes the chicken but also gives it a slight sweetness.

INGREDIENTS

Serves 6

8-ounce can pineapple chunks
1 teaspoon ground cumin
1 teaspoon ground coriander
$^1/_2$ teaspoon crushed garlic
1 teaspoon ground chilies
1 teaspoon salt
2 tablespoons plain yogurt
1 tablespoon chopped fresh cilantro
orange food coloring (optional)
10 ounces chicken, skinned and boned
$^1/_2$ red bell pepper
$^1/_2$ yellow or green bell pepper
1 large onion
6 cherry tomatoes
1 tablespoon vegetable oil

1 Drain the pineapple juice into a bowl. Reserve 8 large chunks of pineapple, squeeze the juice from the remaining chunks into the bowl and set aside. You should have about $^1/_2$ cup pineapple juice.

2 In a large mixing bowl, blend the cumin, ground coriander, garlic, ground chili, salt, yogurt, fresh cilantro and a few drops of food coloring, if using. Pour the reserved pineapple juice into the mixture and stir.

3 Cut the chicken into bite-size cubes, add to the mixing bowl with the yogurt and spice mixture and allow to marinate for about 1–1$^1/_2$ hours.

4 Cut the peppers and onion into bite-size chunks.

COOK'S TIP

If possible, use a mixture of chicken breast and thigh meat for this recipe.

5 Preheat the broiler to medium. Arrange the chicken pieces, peppers, onion, tomatoes and reserved pineapple chunks alternately on 6 wooden or metal skewers.

6 Baste the kebabs with the oil, then place the skewers on a flameproof dish or broiler pan. Broil, turning and basting the chicken pieces with the marinade regularly, for about 15 minutes.

7 Once the chicken pieces are cooked, remove them from the broiler and serve either with salad or plain boiled rice.

Chicken with Spiced Rice

This is a good dish for entertaining. It can be prepared in advance and reheated in the oven. Serve with traditional curry accompaniments.

INGREDIENTS

Serves 8

2 pounds boneless chicken thighs

4 tablespoons olive oil

2 large onions, thinly sliced

1–2 green chilies, seeded and finely
 chopped

1 teaspoon grated fresh ginger

1 garlic clove, crushed

1 tablespoon hot curry powder

$^2/_3$ cup homemade or canned
 chicken stock

$^2/_3$ cup plain yogurt

2 tablespoons chopped fresh cilantro, to
 garnish

salt and black pepper

For the spiced rice

generous $2^1/_4$ cups white basmati rice

$^1/_2$ teaspoon garam masala

$3^3/_4$ cups chicken stock or water

scant $^1/_2$ cup dark or golden raisins

$^1/_2$ cup chopped toasted almonds

1 Put the basmati rice into a sieve and wash under cold running water to remove any starchy powder coating the grains. Then put into a bowl, cover with cold water and let soak for 30 minutes. The grains will absorb some water so that they will not stick together in a solid mass while cooking.

2 Preheat the oven to 325°F. Cut the chicken into bite-size cubes. Heat 2 tablespoons of the oil in a large flameproof casserole, add one onion and cook until softened. Add the finely chopped chilies, grated ginger, crushed garlic and curry powder to the casserole and continue cooking for another 2 minutes, stirring occasionally.

3 Add the stock and seasoning, and bring slowly to a boil. Add the chicken. Cover and bake for 20 minutes, or until tender.

4 Remove from the oven and stir in the yogurt.

5 Meanwhile, heat the remaining oil in a flameproof casserole and cook the remaining onion gently until tender and lightly browned. Add the drained rice, garam masala and stock or water. Bring to a boil, cover and cook in the oven with the chicken for 20–35 minutes, or until the rice is tender and all the stock has been absorbed.

6 To serve, stir the raisins and toasted almonds into the rice. Spoon half the rice into a large deep serving dish, cover with the chicken and then the remaining rice. Sprinkle with chopped cilantro to garnish.

Hot Chicken Curry

This curry has a delicious thick sauce with extra color provided by chunks of red and green pepper.

INGREDIENTS

Serves 4

2 tablespoons corn oil
$^1/_4$ teaspoon fenugreek seeds
$^1/_4$ teaspoon onion seeds
2 onions, chopped
$^1/_2$ teaspoon chopped garlic
$^1/_2$ teaspoon chopped fresh ginger
1 teaspoon ground coriander
1 teaspoon ground chilies
1 teaspoon salt
14-ounce can tomatoes
2 tablespoons lemon juice
$2^1/_2$ cups cubed chicken
2 tablespoons chopped fresh cilantro
3 green chilies, chopped
$^1/_2$ red bell pepper, cut into chunks
$^1/_2$ green bell pepper, cut into chunks
fresh cilantro sprigs, to garnish

1 In a medium saucepan, heat the oil and fry the fenugreek and onion seeds until they turn a shade darker. Add the chopped onions, garlic and ginger and fry for about 5 minutes, until the onions turn golden brown. Reduce the heat to very low.

2 Meanwhile, in a separate bowl, combine the ground coriander, ground chilies, salt, tomatoes and lemon juice.

3 Pour this mixture into the saucepan with the onions and increase the heat to medium. Stir-fry for about 3 minutes.

4 Add the chicken pieces and stir-fry for 5–7 minutes.

5 Add the cilantro, chilies and peppers. Lower the heat, cover and simmer for 10 minutes, until the chicken is cooked.

6 Serve hot, garnished with fresh cilantro sprigs.

COOK'S TIP

For a milder version of this delicious curry, simply omit some or all of the green chilies.

San Francisco Chicken Wings

Make these as spicy as you like – just add more chili sauce.

Serves 4

3/4 cup soy sauce

1 tablespoon light brown sugar

1 tablespoon rice vinegar

2 tablespoons dry sherry

juice of 1 orange

2-inch strip orange rind

1 star anise

1 teaspoon cornstarch

1/4 cup water

1 tablespoon minced fresh ginger

1/4–1 teaspoon Asian chili-garlic
   sauce, to taste

3–31/2 pounds chicken wings, about
   22–24, tips removed

1 Preheat the oven to 400°F. In a saucepan, combine the soy sauce, light brown sugar, rice vinegar, dry sherry, orange juice and rind and star anise. Bring to a boil over a medium heat.

2 Combine the cornstarch and water in a small bowl and stir until blended. Add to the boiling soy sauce mixture, stirring well. Boil for another 1 minute, stirring constantly.

3 Remove the soy sauce mixture from the heat and stir in the minced ginger and chili-garlic sauce to taste.

4 Arrange the chicken wings in one layer in a large baking dish. Pour the soy sauce mixture over them and stir to coat the wings.

5 Bake until tender and browned, 30–40 minutes, basting occasionally. Serve the wings hot or warm.

Fragrant Chicken Curry

*In this dish, the mildly spiced sauce
is thickened using lentils rather than
the traditional onions fried in ghee.*

INGREDIENTS

Serves 4

scant 1/2 cup red lentils

2 tablespoons mild curry powder

2 teaspoons ground coriander

1 teaspoon cumin seeds

2 cups vegetable stock

8 chicken thighs, skinned

8 ounces shredded fresh or thawed frozen
    spinach, well drained

1 tablespoon chopped fresh cilantro

salt and black pepper

fresh cilantro sprigs, to garnish

white or brown basmati rice and
    poppadums, to serve

1 Rinse the lentils under cold
running water. Put into a large,
heavy saucepan with the curry
powder, ground coriander, cumin
seeds and stock.

2 Bring to a boil, then lower the
heat. Cover and simmer gently
for 10 minutes.

3 Add the chicken and spinach.
Cover and simmer gently for
another 40 minutes, or until the
chicken is cooked.

4 Stir in the chopped cilantro
and season to taste. Serve
garnished with cilantro sprigs and
accompanied by the rice and
poppadums.

Spicy Masala Chicken

These chicken pieces are broiled and have a sweet-and-sour taste. They can be served cold with a salad and rice or hot with mashed potatoes.

Serves 6

12 chicken thighs
6 tablespoons lemon juice
1 teaspoon chopped fresh ginger
1 teaspoon chopped garlic
1 teaspoon crushed dried red chilies
1 teaspoon salt
1 teaspoon light brown sugar
2 tablespoons honey
2 tablespoons chopped fresh cilantro
1 green chili, finely chopped
2 tablespoons vegetable oil
fresh cilantro sprigs, to garnish

1 Prick the chicken thighs with a fork, rinse, pat dry and set aside in a bowl.

2 In a large mixing bowl, make the marinade by combining the lemon juice, ginger, garlic, crushed dried red chilies, salt, sugar and honey.

3 Transfer the chicken thighs to the spice mixture and coat well. Set aside for about 45 minutes.

4 Preheat the broiler to medium. Add the cilantro and chopped green chili to the chicken thighs and place them in a flameproof baking dish.

5 Pour any remaining marinade over the chicken and baste with the oil.

6 Broil the chicken thighs under the preheated broiler for 15–20 minutes, turning and basting occasionally, until they are cooked through and browned.

7 Transfer the chicken to a serving dish and garnish with a few sprigs of cilantro.

Tandoori Chicken

A famous Indian/Pakistani chicken dish which is cooked in, and takes its name from, a clay oven called a tandoor, this is extremely popular in the West and appears on the majority of Indian restaurant menus. Though the authentic tandoori flavor is difficult to achieve in conventional ovens, this version still makes a very tasty dish.

INGREDIENTS

Serves 4

4 chicken quarters
3/4 cup plain low-fat yogurt
1 teaspoon garam masala
1 teaspoon chopped fresh ginger
1 teaspoon chopped garlic
1 1/2 teaspoons ground chilies
1/4 teaspoon ground turmeric
1 teaspoon ground coriander
1 tablespoon lemon juice
1 teaspoon salt
a few drops red food coloring
2 tablespoons corn oil

To garnish
mixed lettuce leaves
lime wedges
1 tomato, quartered

2 Stir together the yogurt, garam masala, ginger, garlic, ground chilies, turmeric, ground coriander, lemon juice, salt, red food coloring and oil, and beat until well mixed.

3 Cover the chicken quarters with the yogurt and spice mixture and marinate for about 3 hours.

4 Preheat the oven to 475°F. Transfer the chicken pieces to an ovenproof dish.

5 Bake in the oven for 20–25 minutes, or until the chicken is cooked through and browned on top.

6 Remove from the oven, transfer to a serving dish and garnish with the lettuce leaves, lime and tomato.

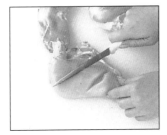

1 Skin, rinse and pat dry the chicken quarters. Make 2 slits in the flesh of each piece, place in a dish and set aside.

Chicken Naan Pockets

This quick and easy dish is ideal for a speedy snack, lunch or supper. To save time, use the ready-to-bake naans available in some super-markets and Asian stores, or try warmed pita bread instead.

INGREDIENTS

Serves 4

4 ready-prepared naans
3 tablespoons plain low-fat yogurt
1¹/₂ teaspoons garam masala
1 teaspoon ground chilies
1 teaspoon salt
3 tablespoons lemon juice
1 tablespoon chopped fresh cilantro
1 green chili, chopped
3¹/₄ cups cubed chicken
1 tablespoon vegetable oil (optional)
8 onion rings
2 tomatoes, quartered
¹/₂ white cabbage, shredded

To garnish
lemon wedges
2 small tomatoes, halved
mixed lettuce leaves
fresh cilantro

1 Cut into the middle of each naan to make a pocket, then set aside.

2 Stir together the yogurt, garam masala, ground chilies, salt, lemon juice, fresh cilantro and chopped green chili. Pour the marinade over the chicken pieces and allow to marinate for about 1 hour.

3 Preheat the broiler to very hot, then lower the heat to medium. Place the chicken in a flameproof dish and broil for 15–20 minutes, until cooked, turning the chicken pieces at least twice.

4 Remove from the heat and fill each naan with the chicken, onion rings, tomatoes and cabbage. Serve with the garnish ingredients.

Chicken Tikka

This chicken dish is an extremely popular Indian appetizer and is quick and easy to cook. Chicken Tikka can also be served as a main course for four.

INGREDIENTS

Serves 6

3¹/₄ cups cubed chicken
1 teaspoon chopped fresh ginger
1 teaspoon chopped garlic
1 teaspoon ground chilies
¹/₄ teaspoon ground turmeric
1 teaspoon salt
²/₃ cup plain low-fat yogurt
4 tablespoons lemon juice
1 tablespoon chopped fresh cilantro
1 tablespoon vegetable oil

To garnish
1 small onion, cut into rings
lime wedges
mixed salad
fresh cilantro

1 In a medium bowl, combine the chicken pieces, ginger, garlic, ground chilies, turmeric, salt, yogurt, lemon juice and fresh cilantro and marinate for at least 2 hours.

2 Place on a broiler pan or in a flameproof dish lined with foil and baste with the oil.

3 Preheat the broiler to medium. Broil the chicken for 15–20 minutes, until cooked, turning and basting two or three times. Serve with the garnish ingredients.

Chicken in Cashew Sauce

This chicken dish has a deliciously thick and nutty sauce, and it is best served with plain boiled rice.

INGREDIENTS

Serves 4

2 onions

2 tablespoons tomato paste

$1/3$ cup cashews

$1^1/2$ teaspoons garam masala

1 teaspoon crushed garlic

1 teaspoon ground chilies

1 tablespoon lemon juice

$1/4$ teaspoon ground turmeric

1 teaspoon salt

1 tablespoon plain low-fat yogurt

2 tablespoons corn oil

1 tablespoon chopped fresh cilantro

1 tablespoon golden raisins

$3^1/4$ cups cubed chicken

$2^1/4$ cups button mushrooms

$1^1/4$ cups water

chopped fresh cilantro, to garnish

1 Cut the onions into quarters, then place them in a food processor or blender and process for about 1 minute.

2 Add the tomato paste, cashews, garam masala, garlic, ground chilies, lemon juice, turmeric, salt and yogurt. Process for another $1–1^1/2$ minutes.

3 In a saucepan, heat the oil, lower the heat to medium and pour in the spice mixture from the food processor. Fry for about 2 minutes, turning down the heat if necessary.

4 Add the fresh cilantro, golden raisins and cubed chicken and continue to stir-fry for 1 minute.

5 Add the mushrooms, pour in the water and bring to a simmer. Cover and cook over low heat for about 10 minutes, or until the chicken is cooked through and the sauce is thick. Cook for a little longer if necessary.

6 Serve garnished with chopped fresh cilantro.

Chicken with Green Mango

Green, unripe mango is used for cooking various dishes on the Indian sub-continent, including pickles, chutneys and some meat, chicken and vegetable dishes. This is a fairly simple chicken dish to prepare and is served with rice and dal.

INGREDIENTS

Serves 4

1 green mango
3¹/4 cups cubed chicken
¹/4 teaspoon black onion seeds
1 teaspoon grated fresh ginger
¹/2 teaspoon crushed garlic
1 teaspoon ground chilies
¹/4 teaspoon ground turmeric
1 teaspoon salt
1 teaspoon ground coriander
2 tablespoons corn oil
2 onions, sliced
4 curry leaves
1¹/4 cups water
2 tomatoes, quartered
2 green chilies, chopped
2 tablespoons chopped fresh cilantro

1 To prepare the mango, peel, pit and slice the flesh thickly. Place the mango slices in a small bowl, cover and set aside.

2 Place the chicken cubes in a bowl and add the onion seeds, ginger, garlic, ground chilies, turmeric, salt and ground coriander. Mix the spices into the chicken and then add half the mango slices.

3 In a medium saucepan, heat the oil and fry the sliced onions until they turn golden brown. Add the curry leaves.

4 Gradually add the spiced chicken pieces and mango slices, stirring constantly.

5 Pour in the water, lower the heat and cook for about 12–15 minutes, stirring occasionally, until the chicken is cooked through and the water has been absorbed.

6 Add the remaining mango slices, the tomatoes, green chilies and cilantro and serve hot.

Karahi Chicken with Mint

For this tasty dish, the chicken is first boiled before being quickly stir-fried in a little oil.

INGREDIENTS

Serves 4

10 ounces chicken breast fillet, skinned
    and cut into strips

1¼ cups water

2 tablespoons soy oil

2 bunches scallions, coarsely chopped

1 teaspoon grated fresh ginger

1 teaspoon crushed dried red chili

2 tablespoons lemon juice

1 tablespoon chopped fresh cilantro

1 tablespoon chopped fresh mint

3 tomatoes, seeded and
    roughly chopped

1 teaspoon salt

mint and cilantro sprigs, to garnish

1 Put the chicken and water into a saucepan, bring to a boil and lower the heat to medium. Cook for about 10 minutes, or until the water has evaporated and the chicken is cooked. Remove from the heat and set aside.

2 Heat the oil in a frying pan or saucepan and stir-fry the scallions for about 2 minutes until soft.

3 Add the boiled chicken strips to the frying pan or saucepan and stir-fry them for about 3 minutes over medium heat.

4 Gradually add the ginger, dried chili, lemon juice, fresh cilantro, fresh mint, tomatoes and salt and gently stir to blend all the flavors together well.

5 Transfer to a serving dish and garnish with the fresh mint and cilantro sprigs.

Karahi Chicken with Fresh Fenugreek

Fresh fenugreek is a flavor that is not widely known. This recipe is a good introduction to this delicious herb.

Serves 4

4 ounces chicken thigh meat,
   skinned and cut into strips

4 ounces chicken breast fillet,
   cut into strips

$1/2$ teaspoon chopped garlic

1 teaspoon ground chilies

$1/2$ teaspoon salt

2 teaspoons tomato paste

2 tablespoons soy oil

1 bunch fenugreek leaves

1 tablespoon chopped fresh
   cilantro

$1^1/4$ cups water

rice or chapatis, to serve

1 Bring a saucepan of water to a boil, add the chicken and cook for 5–7 minutes. Drain.

2 In a mixing bowl, combine the garlic, ground chilies and salt with the tomato paste.

3 Heat the oil in a large saucepan. Lower the heat and add the tomato paste and spice mixture.

4 Add the chicken pieces and stir-fry for 5–7 minutes. Lower the heat again.

5 Add the fenugreek leaves and fresh cilantro. Continue to stir-fry for 5–7 minutes.

6 Pour in the water, cover and cook for about 5 minutes, and serve hot with rice or chapatis.

COOK'S TIP

When preparing fresh fenugreek, use only the leaves and discard the stems, which are very bitter.

Moroccan Chicken Couscous

A subtly spiced and fragrant dish with a fruity sauce.

Serves 4

1 tablespoon butter

1 tablespoon sunflower oil

4 chicken portions, about 6 ounces each

2 onions, finely chopped

2 garlic cloves, crushed

$1/2$ teaspoon ground cinnamon

$1/4$ teaspoon ground ginger

$1/4$ teaspoon ground turmeric

2 tablespoons orange juice

2 teaspoons honey

salt

fresh mint sprigs, to garnish

For the couscous

2 cups couscous

1 teaspoon salt

2 teaspoons sugar

2 tablespoons sunflower oil

$1/2$ teaspoon ground cinnamon

pinch of grated nutmeg

1 tablespoon orange flower water

2 tablespoons golden raisins

$1/2$ cup chopped blanched almonds

3 tablespoons chopped pistachios

1 Heat the butter and oil in a large pan and add the chicken portions, skin-side down. Fry for 3–4 minutes, until the skin is golden, then turn over.

2 Add the onions, garlic, spices and a pinch of salt and pour on the orange juice and $1^{1}/4$ cups water. Cover and bring to a boil, then reduce the heat and simmer for about 30 minutes.

3 Meanwhile, place the couscous and salt in a bowl and cover with $1^{1}/2$ cups water. Stir once and let stand for 5 minutes. Add the sugar, 1 tablespoon of the oil, the cinnamon, nutmeg, orange flower water and golden raisins and mix.

4 Heat the remaining 1 tablespoon oil in a pan and lightly fry the almonds until golden. Stir into the couscous with the pistachios.

5 Line a steamer with waxed paper and spoon in the couscous. Sit the steamer over the chicken (or over a pan of boiling water) and steam for 10 minutes.

6 Remove the steamer and keep covered. Stir the honey into the chicken liquid and boil rapidly for 3–4 minutes. Spoon the couscous onto a warmed serving platter. Top with the chicken, and some of the sauce. Garnish with the fresh mint and serve with the remaining sauce.

Chicken and Chorizo Tacos

Use ready-made taco shells and fill with tasty ground chicken.

Serves 4

1 tablespoon vegetable oil
1 pound ground chicken
1 teaspoon salt
1 teaspoon ground cumin
12 taco shells
3 ounces chorizo sausage, chopped
3 scallions, chopped
2 tomatoes, chopped
1/2 head of lettuce, shredded
2 cups grated Cheddar cheese
tomato salsa, to serve

1 Preheat the oven to 350°F.

2 Heat the oil in a nonstick frying pan. Add the chicken, salt and cumin and fry over medium heat until the chicken is cooked through, 5–8 minutes. Stir frequently to prevent large lumps from forming.

3 Meanwhile, arrange the taco shells in one layer on a large baking sheet and heat in the oven for about 10 minutes, or according to the directions on the package.

4 Add the chorizo and scallions to the chicken and stir to combine. Cook until just warmed through, stirring occasionally.

5 To assemble each taco, place 1–2 spoonfuls of the chicken mixture in the bottom of a warmed taco shell. Top with a generous sprinkling of chopped tomato, shredded lettuce, and grated cheese.

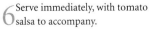

6 Serve immediately, with tomato salsa to accompany.

Chicken Pilaf

This dish is a complete meal in itself, but also makes a good accompaniment to curries.

INGREDIENTS

Serves 4

2 cups basmati rice

6 tablespoons low-fat margarine

1 onion, sliced

$^1/_4$ teaspoon mixed black onion and mustard seeds

3 curry leaves

1 teaspoon grated fresh ginger

1 teaspoon crushed garlic

1 teaspoon ground coriander

1 teaspoon ground chilies

$1^1/_2$ teaspoons salt

2 tomatoes, sliced

1 potato, cubed

$^1/_2$ cup frozen peas

$1^1/_4$ cups cubed chicken

4 tablespoons chopped fresh cilantro

2 green chilies, chopped

3 cups water

1 Wash and soak the rice in cold water for 30 minutes, then set aside in a sieve.

2 In a medium saucepan, melt the low-fat margarine and fry the sliced onion until golden.

3 Add the onion and mustard seeds, the curry leaves, grated ginger, crushed garlic, ground coriander, ground chilies and salt to the saucepan. Stir-fry for about 2 minutes to cook the spices.

4 Add the sliced tomatoes, cubed potato, peas and chicken and mix well.

5 Add the drained rice and stir gently to combine with the other ingredients.

6 Finally, add the fresh cilantro and chopped green chilies. Mix and stir-fry for another minute. Pour in the water.

7 Bring to a boil and lower the heat. Cover and cook for about 20 minutes.

Cajun Chicken

Use ham and shrimp if you have them, but chicken and chorizo sausage are the main ingredients for this dish.

INGREDIENTS

Serves 4
1 chicken, 2¹/2 pounds
1¹/2 onions
1 bay leaf
4 black peppercorns
1 parsley sprig
2 tablespoons vegetable oil
2 garlic cloves, chopped
1 green bell pepper, seeded and chopped
1 stalk celery, chopped
1¹/4 cups long-grain rice
1 cup chorizo sausage, sliced
1 cup chopped cooked ham
14-ounce can chopped tomatoes
   with herbs
¹/2 teaspoon ground chilies
¹/2 teaspoon cumin seeds
¹/2 teaspoon ground cumin
1 teaspoon dried thyme
1 cup cooked peeled shrimp
dash of Tabasco sauce
chopped parsley, to garnish

1 Place the chicken in a large flameproof casserole and add 2¹/2 cups cold water. Add the half onion, the bay leaf, peppercorns and parsley and bring to a boil. Cover and simmer gently for about 1¹/2 hours.

2 When the chicken is cooked, lift it out of the stock, remove the skin and carcass and chop the meat. Strain the stock, allow to cool and reserve.

3 Chop the remaining onion and heat the oil in a large frying pan. Add the onion, garlic, green pepper and celery. Fry for about 5 minutes, then stir in the rice, coating the grains with the oil. Add the sausage, ham and reserved chopped chicken and fry for another 2–3 minutes, stirring frequently.

4 Pour in the tomatoes and 1¹/4 cups of the reserved stock and add the ground chilies, cumin and thyme. Bring to a boil, then cover and simmer gently for 20 minutes, or until the rice is tender and the liquid is absorbed.

5 Stir in the shrimp and Tabasco. Cook for another 5 minutes, then season well and serve hot, garnished with chopped parsley.

Galveston Chicken

A Texas favorite, this crisp-roasted chicken is packed with garlic.

INGREDIENTS

Serves 4

1 chicken, 3–3^1/2 pounds

juice of 1 lemon

4 garlic cloves, crushed

1 tablespoon cayenne pepper

1 tablespoon paprika

1 tablespoon dried oregano

^{1}/2 teaspoon coarse black pepper

2 teaspoons olive oil

1 teaspoon salt

1 With a sharp knife or poultry shears, remove the backbone from the chicken. Turn it breast side up. With the heel of your hand, press down to break the breastbone, and open the chicken flat like a book. Insert a skewer through the chicken, at the thighs, to keep it flat during cooking.

2 Place the chicken in a shallow dish and pour on the lemon juice to coat.

3 In a small bowl, combine the garlic, cayenne, paprika, oregano, pepper and oil. Mix well. Rub evenly over the surface of the chicken.

4 Cover and let marinate 2–3 hours at room temperature, or chill overnight (return to room temperature before roasting).

5 Season the chicken with salt on both sides. Transfer it to a shallow roasting pan.

6 Put the pan in a cold oven and set the temperature to 400°F. Roast until the chicken is done, about 1 hour, turning occasionally and basting with the pan juices. To test, prick with a skewer: the juices should be clear.

COOK'S TIP

Roasting chicken in an oven that has not been preheated produces an especially crispy skin.

Indian Spiced Chicken

*These tender marinated chicken
pieces can be served hot or cold.*

Serves 4

1 chicken, 4–4 1/2 pounds
mixed salad leaves, such as frisée and
    oakleaf lettuce or radicchio, to serve

For the marinade
2/3 cup plain low-fat yogurt
1 teaspoon paprika
2 teaspoons grated fresh ginger
1 garlic clove, crushed
2 teaspoons garam masala
1/2 teaspoon salt
red food coloring (optional)
juice of 1 lemon

1 Cut the chicken into 8 pieces,
using a sharp knife.

2 Combine all the marinade
ingredients in a large non-
reactive dish, add the chicken
pieces to coat and chill for 4 hours
or overnight, to allow the flavors to
penetrate the meat.

3 Preheat the oven to 400°F.
Remove the chicken pieces
from the marinade and arrange
them in a single layer in a large
ovenproof dish. Bake for 30–40
minutes, or until tender. Reserve
the marinade.

4 Baste with a little of the
marinade while cooking.
Arrange on a bed of salad leaves
and serve hot or cold.

Chili Chicken

Serve as a simple supper dish with boiled potatoes and broccoli, or as a party dish with rice.

INGREDIENTS

Serves 4

12 chicken thighs
1 tablespoon olive oil
1 onion, thinly sliced
1 garlic clove, crushed
1 teaspoon ground chilies or 1 dried red
   chili, chopped
14-ounce can chopped tomatoes,
   with their juice
1 teaspoon sugar
15-ounce can kidney beans, drained
salt and black pepper

1 Cut the chicken into large cubes, removing all skin and bones. Heat the oil in a large flameproof casserole and brown the chicken pieces on all sides. Remove with a slotted spoon and keep warm.

2 Add the onion and garlic to the casserole and cook gently until soft. Stir in the ground chilies or chopped dried chili and cook for 2 minutes. Add the tomatoes with their juice, seasoning and sugar. Bring to a boil.

3 Replace the chicken pieces, cover the casserole and simmer for about 30 minutes, until tender.

4 Add the kidney beans and gently cook for another 5 minutes to heat them through before serving.

Red-hot Chicken

A good party dish. The chicken is marinated the night before, so all you have to do on the day is to cook it in a very hot oven and serve with wedges of lemon and a green salad.

INGREDIENTS

Serves 4

1 chicken, 4–4^1/$_2$ pounds, cut into
   8 pieces

juice of 1 large lemon

^{2}/$_3$ cup plain low-fat yogurt

3 garlic cloves, crushed

2 tablespoons olive oil

1 teaspoon ground turmeric

2 teaspoons paprika

1 teaspoon grated fresh ginger or
   ^{1}/$_2$ teaspoon ground ginger

2 teaspoons garam masala

1 teaspoon salt

a few drops red food coloring (optional)

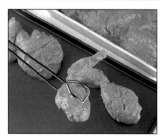

3 Combine the remaining ingredients and pour the sauce over the chicken pieces, turning them to coat thoroughly. Cover with plastic wrap and chill overnight.

4 Preheat the oven to 425°F. Remove the chicken from the marinade and arrange in a single layer on a baking sheet. Bake for 15 minutes, turn over, and cook for another 15 minutes, or until tender.

1 Skin the chicken pieces and cut two slits in each piece.

2 Arrange them in a single layer in a glass or ceramic dish and pour the lemon juice over them.

Chinese Chicken Wings

These are best eaten with fingers as an appetizer. Make sure you provide finger bowls and plenty of paper napkins; things could get messy.

Serves 4

12 chicken wings
3 garlic cloves, crushed
1¹/₂-inch piece fresh ginger, grated
juice of 1 large lemon
3 tablespoons soy sauce
3 tablespoons honey
¹/₂ teaspoon ground chilies
²/₃ cup chicken stock
salt and black pepper
lemon wedges, to garnish

3 Preheat the oven to 425°F. Remove the wings from the marinade and arrange in a single layer in a roasting pan. Bake for 20–25 minutes, basting at least twice with the marinade during cooking.

4 Place the wings on a serving plate. Add the stock to the marinade in the roasting pan, and bring to a boil. Cook to a syrupy consistency and spoon a little over the wings. Serve garnished with lemon wedges.

1 Remove the wing tips and use to make the stock. Cut the wings into two pieces.

2 Combine the remaining ingredients, except for the stock, and coat the chicken pieces in the mixture. Cover with plastic wrap and marinate overnight.

Moroccan Spiced Roast Rock Cornish Hens

Half Rock Cornish game hens served with an apricot and rice stuffing.

INGREDIENTS

Serves 4

generous 1 cup cooked long-grain rice

1 small onion, chopped finely

finely grated rind and juice of 1 lemon

2 tablespoons chopped mint

3 tablespoons chopped dried apricots

2 tablespoons plain yogurt

2 teaspoons ground turmeric

2 teaspoons ground cumin

2 Rock Cornish hens, 1 pound each

salt and black pepper

lemon slices and mint sprigs, to garnish

1 Preheat the oven to 400°F. Combine the rice, onion, lemon rind, mint and apricots. Stir in half each of the lemon juice, yogurt, turmeric, cumin, and salt and pepper.

2 Stuff the birds with the rice mixture at the neck end only. Any spare stuffing can be cooked separately. Place the birds on a rack in a roasting pan.

3 Mix together the remaining lemon juice, yogurt, turmeric and cumin, then brush over the birds. Cover loosely with foil and cook the birds in the oven for 30 minutes.

4 Remove the foil and roast for another 15 minutes, or until golden brown and the juices run clear, not pink, when pierced.

5 Cut the birds in half with a sharp knife or poultry shears, and serve with the spare rice. Garnish with lemon slices and fresh mint sprigs.

Sticky Ginger Chicken

The sweet glaze turns dark and sticky under the broiler or grill.

INGREDIENTS

Serves 4

2 tablespoons lemon juice

2 tablespoons brown sugar

1 teaspoon grated fresh ginger

2 teaspoons soy sauce

8 chicken drumsticks, skinned

black pepper

lettuce and crusty bread, to serve

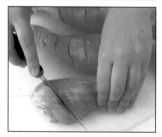

1 Combine the lemon juice, brown sugar, grated ginger, soy sauce and pepper.

2 With a sharp knife, slash the chicken drumsticks about three times through the thickest part, then toss the chicken in the glaze.

3 Cook the chicken drumsticks under a hot broiler or on a barbecue grill, turning occasionally and brushing with the glaze, until the chicken is dark gold and the juices run clear, not pink, when pierced with a skewer. Serve on a bed of lettuce with crusty bread, if you like.

Butterflied Deviled Game Hens

Butterfly *describes very well the idea, if not the actual shape of birds that are split and skewered flat for cooking.*

INGREDIENTS

Serves 4

1 tablespoon powdered English mustard

1 tablespoon paprika

1 tablespoon ground cumin

4 teaspoons ketchup

1 tablespoon lemon juice

5 tablespoons butter, melted

4 Rock Cornish hens, about 1 pound each

salt

2 Using game shears or strong kitchen scissors, split each bird along one side of the backbone, then cut down the other side of the backbone to remove it.

1 Combine the mustard, paprika, cumin, ketchup, lemon juice and salt until smooth, then gradually stir in the butter.

3 Open out a bird, skin side up, then press down firmly with the heel of your hand. Pass a long skewer through one leg and out through the other to secure the bird open and flat. Repeat with the remaining birds.

4 Spread the mustard mixture evenly over the skin of the birds. Cover loosely and put in a cool place for at least 2 hours. Preheat the broiler.

5 Place the birds, skin side up, under the broiler and cook for about 12 minutes. Turn over, baste and cook for another 7 minutes, until the juices run clear.

COOK'S TIP

Butterflied game hens cook well on the barbecue grill. Make sure the coals are hot, then cook for 15–20 minutes, turning and basting frequently.

Sweet-spiced Chicken

Make sure you allow plenty of time for the chicken wings to marinate, so the flavors develop well, then use a wok or a large frying pan for stir-frying.

INGREDIENTS

Serves 4

1 fresh red chili, finely chopped

1 teaspoon ground chilies

1 teaspoon ground ginger

rind of 1 lime, finely grated

12 chicken wings

$^1/_4$ cup sunflower oil

1 tablespoon fresh cilantro, chopped

2 tablespoons soy sauce

$3^1/_2$ tablespoons honey

lime rind and fresh cilantro sprigs,
   to garnish

1 Mix the fresh chili, ground chilies, ground ginger and lime rind together. Rub the mixture into the chicken skins and let sit for at least 2 hours to allow the flavors to penetrate.

2 Heat a wok or large frying pan and add half of the oil. When the oil is hot, add half the wings and stir-fry for 10 minutes, turning frequently until crisp and golden. Drain on paper towels. Repeat with the remaining wings.

3 Add the cilantro to the hot wok and stir-fry for 30 seconds, then return the wings to the wok and stir-fry for 1 minute.

4 Stir in the soy sauce and honey, and stir-fry for 1 minute. Serve the chicken wings hot with the sauce drizzled over them, garnished with lime rind and cilantro sprigs.

Quick Chicken Curry

Curry powder can be bought in three different strengths – mild, medium and hot. Use the type you prefer to suit your taste.

INGREDIENTS

Serves 4

8 chicken legs (thighs and drumsticks)
2 tablespoons vegetable oil
1 onion, thinly sliced
1 garlic clove, crushed
1 tablespoon curry powder
1 tablespoon all-purpose flour
$1^3/4$ cups homemade or canned
   chicken stock
1 beefsteak tomato
1 tablespoon mango chutney
1 tablespoon lemon juice
salt and black pepper

1 Cut the chicken legs in half. Heat the oil in a large flame-proof casserole and brown the chicken pieces on all sides. Remove and keep warm.

2 Add the onion and crushed garlic to the casserole and cook until soft. Add the curry powder and cook gently for 2 minutes.

3 Add the flour, and gradually blend in the chicken stock and the seasoning.

4 Bring to a boil, replace the chicken pieces, cover and simmer for 20–30 minutes, or until tender and cooked through.

5 Blanch the tomato in boiling water for 45 seconds, then run it under cold water to loosen the skin. Peel and cut into small cubes.

6 Add to the chicken, with the mango chutney and lemon juice. Heat through gently and adjust the seasoning to taste.

Chicken in Green Almond Sauce

*This casserole with its spicy sauce
originated in Mexico.*

INGREDIENTS

Serves 6

1 chicken, 3–3½ pounds, cut into
  serving pieces
2 cups homemade or canned
  chicken stock
1 onion, chopped
1 garlic clove, chopped
2 cups coarsely chopped fresh cilantro
1 green bell pepper, seeded and chopped
1 *jalapeño* pepper, seeded and chopped
10-ounce can tomatillos (Mexican green
  tomatoes)
1 cup ground almonds
2 tablespoons corn oil
salt
fresh cilantro sprig, to garnish
rice, to serve

1 Put the chicken pieces in a
flameproof casserole or shallow
pan. Pour in the stock, bring to a
simmer, cover and cook for about
45 minutes, until tender. Drain
the stock into a measuring cup and
set aside.

2 Put the onion, garlic, cilantro,
green and *jalapeño* peppers,
tomatillos with their juice, and the
almonds in a food processor. Purée
fairly coarsely.

3 Heat the oil in a frying pan,
add the almond mixture and
cook over low heat, stirring with a
wooden spoon, for 3–4 minutes.
Scrape into the casserole or pan
with the chicken.

4 If necessary, add water to the
stock to make 2 cups. Stir it
into the casserole or pan. Mix
gently and simmer just long
enough to blend the flavors
and heat the chicken pieces
through. Add salt to taste. Serve
immediately, garnished with
cilantro and accompanied by rice.

COOK'S TIP

If the color of the sauce seems a
little pale, add 2–3 outer leaves of
dark green Romaine lettuce. Cut
out the central vein, chop the
leaves and add at step 2.

Chicken Bobotie

Perfect for a buffet party, this mild curry dish is set with savory custard, which makes serving easy. Serve with boiled rice and chutney.

INGREDIENTS

Serves 8

two thick slices white bread

1³/4 cups milk

2 tablespoons olive oil

2 medium onions, finely chopped

3 tablespoons medium curry powder

2¹/2 pounds ground chicken

1 tablespoon apricot jam, chutney or sugar

2 tablespoons wine vinegar or lemon juice

3 large eggs, beaten

¹/3 cup dark or golden raisins

12 whole almonds

salt and black pepper

3 Mash the bread in the milk and add to the pan with one of the beaten eggs and the raisins.

4 Grease a 6-cup shallow ovenproof dish with butter. Spoon in the chicken mixture and level the top. Cover with buttered foil and bake in the oven for 30 minutes.

5 Meanwhile, beat the remaining eggs and milk. Remove the dish from the oven and lower the temperature to 300°F. Break up the meat using a fork and pour the egg mixture on top.

6 Scatter on the almonds and bake, uncovered, for 30 minutes until set and brown.

1 Preheat the oven to 350°F. Soak the bread in ²/3 cup of the milk. Heat the oil in a frying pan and gently fry the onions until tender then add the curry powder and cook for another 2 minutes.

2 Add the ground chicken and brown all over, separating the grains of meat as they brown. Remove from the heat and season with salt and black pepper. Add the apricot jam, chutney or sugar and the wine vinegar or lemon juice.

Chicken Biryani

*A deceptively easy curry to make,
and very tasty, too.*

INGREDIENTS

Serves 4

1 1/2 cups basmati rice, rinsed

1/2 teaspoon salt

5 whole cardamom pods

2–3 whole cloves

1 cinnamon stick

3 tablespoons vegetable oil

3 onions, sliced

4 chicken breasts, 6 ounces each, cubed,
    skinned and boned

1/4 teaspoon ground cloves

5 cardamom pods, seeds removed and
    ground

1/4 teaspoon ground chilies

1 teaspoon ground cumin

1 teaspoon ground coriander

1/2 teaspoon black pepper

3 garlic cloves, finely chopped

1 teaspoon finely chopped fresh ginger

juice of 1 lemon

4 tomatoes, sliced

2 tablespoons chopped fresh cilantro

2/3 cup plain yogurt

1/2 teaspoon saffron strands soaked in
    2 teaspoons hot milk

3 tablespoons toasted slivered almonds
    and fresh cilantro sprigs, to garnish

plain yogurt, to serve

1 Preheat the oven to 375°F.
Bring a pan of water to a boil
and add the rice, salt, cardamom
pods, cloves and cinnamon stick.
Boil for 2 minutes and then drain,
leaving the whole spices in the rice.

2 Heat the oil in a pan and fry
the onions for 8 minutes, until
browned. Add the chicken
followed by all the ground spices,
the garlic, ginger and lemon juice.
Stir-fry for 5 minutes.

3 Transfer the chicken mixture
to a casserole and lay the sliced
tomatoes on top. Sprinkle on the
cilantro, spoon on the plain yogurt
and top with the drained rice.

4 Drizzle the saffron and milk
over the rice and pour on
2/3 cup of water.

5 Cover tightly and bake in the
oven for 1 hour. Transfer to a
warmed serving platter and
remove the whole spices from the
rice. Garnish with toasted almonds
and cilantro and serve with extra
plain yogurt.

Index